Myron Oygold

Social Fictions series

Series Editor
Patricia Leavy, PhD
USA

The *Social Fictions* series emerges out of the arts-based research movement. The series includes full-length fiction books that are informed by social research but written in a literary/artistic form (novels, plays, and short story collections). Believing there is much to learn through fiction, the series only includes works written entirely in the literary medium adapted. Each book includes an academic introduction that explains the research and teaching that informs the book as well as how the book can be used in college courses. The books are underscored with social science or other scholarly perspectives and intended to be relevant to the lives of college students—to tap into important issues in the unique ways that artistic or literary forms can.

Please email queries to pleavy7@aol.com

Myron Oygold

A Graduate Student Struggles

Jason Matthew Zalinger

SENSE PUBLISHERS
ROTTERDAM/BOSTON/TAIPEI

A C.I.P. record for this book is available from the Library of Congress.

ISBN: 978-94-6351-123-0 (paperback)
ISBN: 978-94-6351-124-7 (hardback)
ISBN: 978-94-6351-125-4 (e-book)

Published by: Sense Publishers,
P.O. Box 21858,
3001 AW Rotterdam,
The Netherlands
https://www.sensepublishers.com/

All chapters in this book have undergone peer review.

Printed on acid-free paper

ADVANCE PRAISE FOR
MYRON OYGOLD: A GRADUATE STUDENT STRUGGLES

"*Myron Oygold: A Graduate Student Struggles* is simultaneously quirky and funny, yet achingly sad. Zalinger's stories are both deeply intimate and strikingly universal in the emotions they evoke. His work conjures the sentiment of Phillip Roth and the postmodern mischief of Thomas Pynchon. Myron Oygold is a memorable character, ensconced by despair yet existing in technologically mediated moments of joy and hope."
– Shira Chess, Assistant Professor of Entertainment and Media Studies, University of Georgia

"I went to school with Jason Zalinger. I knew he was demented, but I never know how demented. Now I do, and I don't know if I ever want to go back. Often dark, at times scary, humorous, and scathing, but always thoughtful, Zalinger's prose flies off the page. Reading his stories brought back memories of school but also memories of fear. Like a trip into Freud's nightmare. After reading these stories, you'll know what it was like to go to school with Zalinger as well. And God help us all."
– Paul Booth, Associate Professor of Media and Cinema Studies/ Communication Technology, DePaul University

To my niece, Olivia

TABLE OF CONTENTS

PREFACE

Looking behind my TV, I see a tangle of wires. Over the years, as more wires and devices are added and plugged in, they seem to fuse together. This is how I think of relationships. They are like the wires behind your TV. They don't start that way. It begins with one little TV. One little cord plugged in. *I love you.* Then, years go by, more wires. More plugs. And one day you look back there and think, *how did we get here?*

How do we make sense of our tangled, messy lives? How do we make sense of love or death? How do we make sense of joy, sadness, and anxiety? How do we make sense of fear? How can we honestly explain the *decisions* we have made?

The answer is that we tell stories. Stories are how we make sense of the complex emotional calculus that motivates our decisions. Math cannot explain love lost. But maybe if I tell you a story, you will understand me. And isn't that the goal? That somehow, someway, other humans understand us? This desperate desire for connection is deeply ingrained in us. Stories are the buckets that contain the just-barely-spilling-over stuff of life. We haul these heavy buckets around, stories splashing out and splattering on the pavement, looking for anyone who will listen. We live inside of a story we are furiously writing, the pen just ahead of us, scribbling the bridges that sustain us from falling into some lonely abyss.

German philosopher Wilhelm Dilthey said that slowly, over time, we experience a "coming-together-of-a-life." Meaning, organically our lives somehow coalesce (qtd. in Kearney, p. 4). *Myron Oygold* is a collection of linked stories that express a coming-together-of-a-PhD-life, sort of.

Myron Oygold is a chain-smoking, Xanax-popping PhD student trying desperately to finish his doctorate, find lost love, and make something out of his life. Myron's heart and mind were broken by Ilana Berkowitz as their lives exploded in a mushroom cloud of love and pain. Still reeling from the fallout, Myron begins his PhD in

Applied General Studies at Rensselaer Polytechnic Institute. He's not sure why he's there or what he's doing, but he knows Ilana has moved nearby in Albany, and he thinks he can make some meaning out of his life and find again what he lost in the War of D.C.

However, finishing a PhD is hard for an anxious, neurotic guy like Myron. He encounters many obstacles: His adviser, Dr. Samuel Flagson who takes research money from the Department of Defense and Starbucks, a mysterious programmer named Mushi Berger, who works in the Department of Secret Computer Science, the surreal iBaby with whom Myron falls in love, a brilliant, talking chipmunk, a Wikipedia conspiracy, and even a therapist named Carl—sent from God in Myron's time of need. Can Myron ever let go of the past? Can he learn to say what he needs to say? Will he finish his PhD? Will he find again the love he felt in New Haven?

Maybe the most important question for Myron is: Why is he getting a PhD? In fact, why does anyone? I did not set out to tell the "truth" about getting a PhD. I only hope to tell the emotional truth, as I felt it. Myron's story is not my story, exactly. In Myron, I only tried to capture the way I *felt* just before and in graduate school. I sense that graduate school is often a refugee camp for smart, confused people who don't know what else to do. So they show up, fall after fall. Seeking intellectual nourishment because in the real world they feel like they are starving.

And what, exactly, does it *feel* like during that first PhD semester? For me, it felt exciting, chaotic, and stressful. For the first time in my life, I doubted myself. I doubted why I was there or what I was doing. I considered leaving. I applied to MFA programs. *Am I in the wrong place? What am I doing here?* I wondered. My family and friends from home certainly had no idea what I was doing. I think these are common questions and fears but not much talked about. What kept me going were my grad student friends and the incredible *intellectual energy* that tends to radiate out of the grad student beehive. That energy is addictive. It kept me nourished.

I don't know how I can capture the *feeling* of getting a PhD without writing stories. I don't claim to speak for anyone else. I'm sure there are many students who go to graduate school with focused plans, some kind of strategy. Not me. I was a disaster coming in, and I was a disaster squirting out the other end. I was toothpaste, and I put myself in my own tube. I had hoped, my whole life, that someone, somewhere would mentor and shape me, help guide my indefatigable energies into the shape of an arrow, a laser of knowledge, singularly focused on…something. No. I had to squeeze myself, with help from many wonderful professors and friends. But in the end, we all have to squeeze ourselves. Similarly, Myron is trying to squeeze himself. Trying to move forward. Trying to say what he needs to say to the world, to himself. He flounders about. He chain-smokes. He reeks of anxiety. He eats Xanax as if they were Skittles. He wears his "safety outfit" of sweatpants and New Haven t-shirt and North Face wool hat like a shield against the world.

In writing this preface, I took a break to go outside and have a smoke. I saw a first-semester PhD student outside puffing on one of those electronic cigarettes. "How's your first year been"? I ask. He takes an electronic puff and says, "I don't know. I guess this is what I signed up for."

I wrote these stories for him. They are written for all the first-year PhD students wondering, like Myron, why they are doing what they are doing. Like Myron, I know that student will succeed. I know he will have many challenges, and I know that, in the end, it will be worth it.

These stories are written for any first-year graduate student in any field, though first-semester PhDs may find them particularly appealing. They are meant to provoke discussion, to provide a diving board into the deep end, to get students—and faculty—to question why they are doing what they are doing. They are also stories that can be read, I hope, by anyone for pleasure.

Like getting a PhD, like the wires behind a TV, these stories are messy, and yet, there is a coming-together of Myron's life—I think. In the end, now that I've had a few years to reflect. I can honestly say that it is a privilege to do what I do for a living. Getting a PhD is risky and challenging, but in the end, it is worth it. I can only hope that first-year students, filled with excitement and fear, will find some solace in Myron's emotional life. And I sincerely hope they will be more honest with themselves than Myron.

REFERENCE

Kearney, R. (2002). *On stories*. New York, NY: Routledge.

ACKNOWLEDGEMENTS

All I've ever wanted to do was be a fiction writer. Therefore, I want to first thank Series Editor Patricia Leavy for believing in this project. I would also like to thank publisher Peter de Liefde and the rest of the Sense team. Thank you for hanging in there with me. I want to especially thank Shira Chess and Wes Unruh, who were the first people in my life to encourage-force me to write. This book would not be possible without your support. Thank you to all my friends from RPI who read these stories while I was first writing them, Paul Booth, Elia Desjardins, Eric Newsom, Hillary Savoie, David Bello, Amber Davisson, and, of course, Macey Davisson. Additionally, I'd like to thank James P. Zappen, Audrey Bennett, and Nathan Freier for guiding me through my doctorate with wisdom and kindness. I promise these stories are not about you. Thank you to Carolyn Ellis and Art Bochner for their unwavering support over these last few years. I am forever grateful to my parents, Alife and Marilyn Zalinger, for their unconditional love and support no matter what paths I seem to wander down. Finally, I want to thank my little sister, Allison Nelson, who loved Myron from the beginning.

THE ISLAND BEFORE PHD SCHOOL

This is how I remember it. We were in our little one-bedroom apartment on the corner of 15th and P Street in Washington, D.C. I was lying on my side of the bed wearing only a faded, navy-blue t-shirt that said New Haven in white letters and my brown, North Face wool cap. Ilana Berkowitz lay next to me on her side. She was wearing only a navy-blue t-shirt that said Yale in white letters. Her body was slender, her hair black. She had a beautiful Jewish nose. We were looking at each other.

"What do you want?" I asked gently, touching my index finger to the fabric of her t-shirt, careful not to touch her skin.

"I don't know," she said.

"Do you love me?" I said.

"Yes."

"Don't lie." I said.

"I'm not."

"Are you a baby?" I said.

"Are *you* a baby?" she asked, and licked my nose.

"Yeck! Yes, I'm a baby!" I cried, and pulled the blanket up to my lips. Then she said, "Can I rest my head on your belly?"

"I *knew* you were going to ask that!" I said.

"You did?"

"Of course."

For the first time in five months, she rested her long, black hair on my stomach. She once told me that she had always felt my little potbelly was the safest, warmest spot in the world. She told me she would listen to me breathe in and out and imagine she could *see* my energy, my love for her. She said she always imagined it as a little blue ball of energy, pulsing. Now here I was, suddenly given a glimpse of how things used to feel on those rainy Saturday evenings in New

Haven during the fall. Those lovely nights when Ilana returned home from her shift at Yorkside Pizza and immediately unzip me, leaving her calzone to rotate in the microwave.

Now I felt calm as my belly moved up and down with each breath. The minutes piled up like the clank of gold coins. Surprised by my luck, I became greedy. "Ilana?"

"Oh, God!" She knew what I was going to ask.

"No, Ilana… shhh."

"You want me to touch it, don't you?" she said.

"Yes!" I said. Ilana considered this. She breathed slowly. She closed her eyes.

"Okay."

I couldn't believe it. It had been almost a full year since Ilana began to change. One day I was sitting in the rocking chair I had bought her. A surprise gift. I had painted it myself. Pink. Her favorite color. It came out awful, but she cherished it. I was reading *Siddhartha* because Ilana loved it so much, and I had said, "I want to read every book you've read, so I can really *know* you." I rocked calmly. The sun had shifted behind me, and it illuminated the pages. I felt like I was reading through a magnifying glass. Each word seemed big and beautiful and filled with wisdom. I rocked on the hardwood floor. I began to meditate like Siddhartha. I rocked in rhythm to my breath. I felt the sun on the top of my head. Suddenly, Ilana burst in the door ranting about someone at Yorkside. She never hollered. She was always so gentle. But now she was yelling and thrashing about the kitchen. She slammed her calzone into the trash. Then, with her palm, she *pushed* it down like a compactor. She walked to the bedroom. Stopped. She turned to me and said, "I'm sorry, baby." I saw tears in her eyes. When she closed the bedroom door, I realized that *Siddhartha* had fallen to the floor, and I had stopped mid-rock, my calves tensed.

The therapists listened. Counselors talked. The psychologists did very little. The psychiatrists prescribed and prescribed all the usual pills. Nothing. Ilana became more and more withdrawn. She stopped going outside. She stopped leaving the bedroom. She just stopped. The last doctor said to me, "She's slowly becoming a glass table and

the legs are going. One. Two. Three… Maybe we should let her break."
I cried and cried and gave up on the doctors and thought maybe, with
enough time and love, I could fix her.

Now, for the first time in almost a year, she touched it.

"It's so small!" she said jokingly.

"Oh, God!"

"It's okay, Baby."

"I'm just nervous," I said. "It's been so long."

"Myron, baby. I love you. I love *it*. It's mine. It's *my* little thingy."
Ilana was playful again, just like back in New Haven before it all started.
Back in our little apartment on Chapel Street above Book Trader Café.
I loved that place. We would eat chicken Marsala and drink red wine at
The Hot Tomato, then take a little trip to the sex shop on College Street.

"Oh, God," I said.

"I love you. I love your thingy."

My thingy grew.

"I love you, too."

My thingy grew and grew.

"Ilana, oh Ilana, I love you."

"I don't *feel* loved," she suddenly said.

She made tweezers with her fingers. "Don't fuck with me. I'll
pinch it."

"No! Bad Baby!"

My thingy went soft.

"I'll snip it off."

"No! Bad!"

"Snip, snip!"

She propped herself up then thrust a dry finger between my
legs. My eyes illuminated like a red light.

"Bad!" I said.

"Bad?" She eased. I loosened. Yellow light. My thingy grew.

"Good," I said.

"Good now?" she said.

"Good, good baby." Green light. I came like a rabbit, twitchy
small game. I flipped her over, eyes closed, legs like a V. I touched her
down there. She bridled like a horse.

"Slow," she said. Yellow light. I waited. I heard someone whistling down on the sidewalk. I touched her again down there.

"Stop!" she said, and held out her hand. Red light. I waited and waited. Sunlight faded.

All down the avenue, street lamps turned on one by one. I lay next to her. She tapped the comforter with one finger as if it were a piano key. Eventually, she closed her eyes and fell asleep. I got up, lit a cigarette, and wrote in my journal, *You who would steer me into the rocks talking about love in my ear.* She neighed in her sleep. The journal clapped shut. I slid it under the dresser, next to my graduate school applications.

When I got home from work the next evening, she was still asleep. I sang in her ear, "Ilana? Baby? You hungry? Eat some food."

She moaned, woke up, refused to eat. "I have to pee."

"So pee, Baby."

"No." I closed my eyes, rubbed the back of my neck.

"Why?"

"I'm not leaving the bed."

"Baby, go use the bathroom."

"I'll never leave the bed again." She forced me to fetch a deep baking pan. She filled it to the top. I put on a glove and tossed it into the dumpster outside. Walking back up the stairs, I thought *what am I doing?* I wanted to call my mom. I washed my hands and started to microwave dinner.

"Where are you?" she said.

"In the kitchen, Ilana."

"Lay down with me." *What is happening?* I breathed in slowly then exhaled as if I were smoking a cigarette.

"I'd love to, but we have to eat."

"Just for a minute." I sighed, put the pizza back in the freezer, and lay next to her. "Will you take off your pants?" I took them off. She snuggled next to me. She sniffed my hair, rubbed my belly. My stomach grumbled. "I'm sorry, Baby. That was my stomach."

"I didn't hear anything," she said. After a while she fell asleep. I slid quietly out of bed and went to the kitchen. I put the pizza back in the microwave. It began to rotate. Suddenly, she cried out, "Where did you go!"

"Ilana, I'm in the kitchen." *Not one minute to myself!*

"Don't leave me."

"I'm *not* leaving you." *Please!*

"Don't be mad!"

"I'm not mad. I'm hungry." *Please someone help me!*

"Come to bed."

"I'll be there soon."

"Come to bed."

"I'll be there soon."

"Please. Just for a minute." Exasperated, I went to her. "Don't leave me," she said.

"I won't, Ilana." I sat on the edge of the bed as she curled around me like a horseshoe. Outside, I heard the hydraulics of a bus stopping or going. It grew darker, and the microwave went "ding." She curled tighter around me. I sighed as the street lights went on up and down the block. My stomach rumbled. I ran my fingers through her soft, black hair. I could smell the pizza. The microwave dinged again. She curled tighter around me, and I let her.

It took me a whole day of begging to get her to use the bathroom on her own. She refused to shower, so I had to clean her with a damp sponge. "Not down there. Don't touch me down there," she said. I brushed her teeth while she lay in bed. She spat in a coffee mug. She called me at work. "When are you coming home? Do you love me? Where are you? What time is it? I'm asleep. When are you coming home?" I smiled when I had to, finished my work as quickly as I could, and left six minutes early, fifteen minutes, twenty-two...

Two weeks later, after work, I collapsed on the bed. "Baby, I saw a job in the paper today. It's a good job. You'd get benefits. Do you want to—"

"No!"

"Ilana, it's—"

"No!" She pulled the blanket over her head and mumbled underneath, "No, no, no, no nonono!" I curled up next to her and put my hand on her rising and falling belly and wept so that she would not hear. Suddenly she leapt to her feet. She bounced up and down on the bed, causing it to squeak and squeal. She pounded on the wall. "No, no, no!"

"Ilana, what's wrong!"

"No, no, no, nonono!" I jumped up. It was hard to keep balance as she bounced. I put a hand on the wall and a hand on her. She pushed me away. "Get off!"

I shrieked, "Oh, God! Ilana, please tell me what's wrong!"

"I hate it here! I hate it here!"

"Why?"

"I *hate*!" and she slapped the wall as if it were a cheek.

"Why? What happened?"

"Everyone is evil!"

"Who!"

"All of *them*!" She pointed to the window and the cars and cabs driving by and the people walking along the sidewalk. I thought about how much different it looked than Chapel Street. The light was wrong. The cars were wrong. The people were wrong. I reached out to touch her cheek. "Baby, please." She swatted at my fingers as if they were bees. I collapsed on the bed and began to cry.

"Ilana," I whimpered. "Tell me what's wrong."

"I love you!" she screamed.

"I love you too."

"I love you!"

"Ilana, stop."

"Love you!" she screamed and jumped up and down, pointing at me. "You, you, you!"

"Please."

"You don't love me!"

"I do. I love you. I love you so much."

"You don't *love* me!"

"I do. I love you."

"Liar!"

"Baby, please."

"Don't lie to me!"

"Ilana..." I could say no more. Tears choked me like fingers around my neck. She jumped up and down, screamed, and pounded the wall until she exhausted herself. She lay down, facing me, sweat dripping down her nose. I reached over. "Baby?" She closed her eyes, and I kissed her glistening forehead. "Ilana?" She turned over, and I cuddled up next to her. I whispered, "I love you."

"No, you don't."

"Please."

"*Please*," she mimicked.

"I love you."

"Love you."

"I love you."

"No, you don't."

The moon rose over the city and stayed in the sky for two whole days. Streetlights failed. Electricity vanished. Shadows whispered inside shadows. In darkness, we slept the whole time. The bed became a boat, floating farther out than either of us had ever been before. Shark fins circled the bed. She whispered in my ear. I peeled off like Velcro, sat cross-legged and touched the wet shark fins. Eyes shut, she moaned, "Why don't you *hold* me?" The bed picked up speed. It ripped over whitecaps like a buzz-saw, our hair wild in the wind. The fins fell behind, following in formation. The bed slammed into the shore of a little island. I strained my back, dragging the mattress onto the sand. I gathered kindling, flicked my lighter, and made a little fire on the beach. We camped out. She slept, and shadows danced on her illuminated face. I watched her sleep, her stomach rising and falling, and I thought she looked so beautiful. She moaned like an old woman. I thought I might cry but instead rose to my feet and screamed over the black water, "We are dying! I have failed! But I have so much love!" An echo screamed back at me, "Love, love, love!" I fell to my knees and wept. She moaned. The echoes roared like police sirens flashing past us, "Love, love, *love*!" I wept, and my tears sizzled on the sand like beads of water on a stove. She moaned like a patient in a hospital bed, and the moan mixed with the engine-echo roar of "Love, love, *love*!" I curled up next to her, kissed her hot cheek, rubbed her belly, and whispered in her ear, "Baby, little baby. You're a little baby, a little baby..."

***

In the morning, the sun rose bright and clear. While she slept, I slid out, put on my shoes outside the door, and took the bus to Doctor Greenberg's. "Hello, my friend!" he bellowed. "Sit down!" The only place to sit was a metal folding chair, so I sat. He rested his feet on his large oak desk and reclined in a black executive chair. "You probably never thought you'd end up here!"

One night, months before, after I had gotten Ilana to bed, I quietly set my laptop on the kitchen table and searched for help. I didn't know where to begin, so I started typing in Ilana's symptoms. I worried that Ilana would wake up and accuse me of looking at porn, accuse me of searching online dating profiles, so I typed lightly, as if each key were a landmine. A few hours later, lost in a deep maze of links that took me around the world, I was about to give up. Exhausted and desperate, I typed in the word "help." The first link was to a local forum about co-dependency. I began to read, thinking the whole time, *It's not co-dependency. She's the one dependent on* me! Someone had created a thread called DR. GREENBERG SAVED ME! I clicked and read the postings. One man gave an account of his wife that sounded just like Ilana. He claimed that Dr. Greenberg had access to pills not on the market, and that they had cured her. The next person claimed that Dr. Greenberg's pills made her husband even worse and that they ended up in the emergency room. It went back and forth like this. Thirty-six posts. Some claiming he was a genius. Others called him a quack handing out dangerous medications. One even said he had lost his medical license. I thought it over for months. But Ilana was only getting worse. Finally, I decided to make an appointment.

"No," I said, "I never thought I would be here."

"Life is weird," he said, smiling. His teeth were very white and straight. His beard was dark and well-groomed. His hair was black but seemed a little disheveled.

"I never planned on this," I said, holding my arms together as if I were cold.

"Plans change."

"I had it all mapped out," I said, noticing there were no diplomas on the white walls, no bookshelves. Nothing on his desk.

"I bought a map once, and it was all wrong. North was left. West was up. East was missing."

"How did you find your way?"

"I guessed," Dr. Greenberg said and laughed. He took his feet down from his oak desk. He leaned forward in his black chair. He began to rub his stomach, just a little.

"Does your stomach hurt?" I asked.

"No, my friend. The stomach is where your energy is stored. It's my life force!" he said. I could not tell if his smile was terrible or wise, but I liked the idea that a person's energy was contained within their stomach. It reminded me of how Ilana used to say she loved my "little belly," how safe she felt laying her head on it. At least back in New Haven. Wise or terrible. I could not decide, but I loved Ilana, so I let it go.

"Are you happy?" I asked.

"No! Of course not!"

"That doesn't make me feel better."

"What used to make you feel better?"

"When I took her to synagogue, in the rain," I said.

"Are you Jewish?"

"I'm the worst Jew ever."

"Are you very religious?"

"I only pray when I'm in trouble."

"Do you believe in God?" he said.

"I'm afraid not to."

"If you believe in yourself, is that religion?" he said.

"Am I my own God?"

"Maybe God is a kitten I can pet for eternity," Doctor Greenberg said, and made a little petting motion in the air.

"Ilana told me God created the little soft spot under my nose," I said, letting myself go deeper and deeper.

"When a wave splashes against a rock and the spray leaps up to the sun, that is God," he said.

"When a young mother dies alone, and no one hears her last word, that is the devil," I said, thinking of Ilana's mother. She was thirty-five when they moved her to the nursing home. Sickness stripped her beauty like a paint scrapper.

"When a girl falls in love with a boy, and the boy does not love the girl, it's a warning," he said, raising an eyebrow.

"But I *do* love her," I said. *I do love her.*

"When they get drunk and have sex, the devil lights their cigarettes," he said.

"When the devil makes a father touch his daughter, God makes it rain somewhere in the world," I said, thinking of that bastard.

"God smiles," he said.

"And the Devil will pace," I said, and glanced at the floor. Then I looked up and said, "She saved my life. She showed me love."

"There are so many shows."

"We loved so hard, so fast," I said.

"Love doesn't have to be so hard."

"In the winter, I bought her warm socks," I said, thinking of that first December in New Haven, laying on my back and watching snow fall through the window as Ilana's head moved up and down with such love and delicacy.

"My ex-wife spooned me chicken broth all through the blizzard of '77."

"When it rained, I lit candles," I said, thinking of our first summer, how it seemed to rain every Saturday, how we began to *hope* for the rain, so we could lay in bed all day, listen to the rain hit the sidewalk, and twist the sheets.

"I paced for three days, threatened to move to Florida, of all places."

"Last year, I knew everything," I said.

"She knew how to arouse me with a finger," he said.

"Now I have so many questions."

"Question and answer are this far apart," he said and made a "C" with his thumb and index finger.

"Sometimes they're *this* far apart," I said and stretched my arms wide.

"In the end, all we can do is tell stories about the beginning."

"Now she moans in her sleep."

"We wrap the past around us like blankets."

"She won't leave the bed."

"When she left, I carried a pair of her underwear in my pocket for two months."

"I feed her M&M'S from a spoon."

"I remember naps together on Sundays in old apartments in October."

"Her fingernails are bloody. I don't know why."

"It's as if God tilted the table and our lives slid into the trash."

"Can you help me?" Doctor Greenberg opened his desk drawer, withdrew a bottle with no label, and held it out for me to take. I sighed like an old man. I thought about what the people on the forum had said. I looked at my watch. I knew Ilana would be waiting for me, ready to pounce.

"She doesn't like swallowing pills," I said.

"Ah, the pills, the pills roll down your throat like quarters in a vending machine!" he said, shaking the bottle a little. I could hear them rattle.

"How many do I give her?"

"As many as she needs. Take a few for yourself, if you want."

"Really?"

"Sure, what the hell!"

"What do you think is wrong with her?

Dr. Greenberg placed the pill bottle on the oak table.

"What do *you* think is wrong with her?" he said.

I thought about this. Then I said, "What do the pills do?"

"Ah," he said and leaned back in his black chair, rubbing his belly, "They make it so you can say what needs to be said."

While on the bus, it began to rain. I sat alone clutching the bottle like brass knuckles. I looked out the window. A bird rushed through the gloom.

At home, I placed a delicate hand on the doorknob and sighed. Gripping the bottle like a talisman, I twisted the knob and opened the door. "Where were you?" she called from the bedroom. My stomach began to hurt.

"Someplace good," I said.

"You said you would be right back." I still had not entered.

"You were asleep when I left."

"I thought you wouldn't leave." I tightened my grip on the pills.

"I'm here now," I said.

"You said you wouldn't leave me."

"I won't leave you." I stepped inside, but I didn't want to.

"Don't leave."

"I'm not leaving." I sighed. "Ilana, I've got something for you."

"What?"

"The doctor gave it to me." I went to the kitchen and got a spoon. Then I went into the bedroom. She was lying on the bed, on her side. I got down on my knees. I held up the spoon in one hand, then the bottle so she could see. I tapped once. Twice. A small, blue pill rolled out. I said, "Oh, Baby! It's a little blue one. Like an M&M!"

"A little blue one?"

"Yes, Ilana." I patted her head. "Open up, baby girl!"

"No."

"Please?"

"No," she said and closed her eyes.

I closed my eyes, too. I sucked a deep breath into my mouth then exhaled. "I'll take one first." She opened her eyes wide, like those of a child watching a magician at a birthday party. I put the spoon to my mouth. The pill rolled onto my tongue and down my throat. I swallowed without water. "See, Baby? It's good." I tapped another little blue pill onto the spoon. She leaned over, sniffing it like a hound. She crinkled her face as if smelling garbage.

"It's gross!"

"Ilana, no."

"It stinks!"

"It doesn't smell at all."

"It stinks like pee!"

"No, Baby."

"It stinks like poo!"

"Ilana, shhh."

"I won't take it!"

"Do this for me. Please."

"Why?"

"Because I love you."

She turned her back to me. She thrashed around the covers, tossing all four pillows to the ground. She flipped onto her stomach and banged her face into the mattress so that the bed trembled. I, however, began to feel dreamy.

"Ilana, I feel so good." She stopped mid-face-smash.

"What does it feel like?" she said.

"Like floating naked in a pool."

"Like the time we went swimming in the hotel pool when my mom died?" she asked.

"Just like that, except better." She sat up in the bed. She leaned over and kissed my forehead.

"How do you feel now?" she said. I grinned.

"I'm not afraid," I said. I tapped out a pill for her, and it rolled down her throat just like the doctor said. "See, Baby? Just like an M&M." I rolled another down my throat and tapped out another for her. We were quiet for a long time. We lay in bed together, like gingerbread cookies on a pan, smiling, fingers baking together.

"Baby," I said, "How do you feel?"

"Everything is gonna be okay," she said, and we floated into dreams on our little boat bed, and we slept with gingerbread smiles for three days and nights.

Two months ran past our little apartment like a pack of barking dogs chasing a kitten, yet we heard nothing. Each day, I tapped out a little blue pill and watched it roll down her tongue and down her throat. She slept less and less. She began to say nice things to me. "You look nice. I like your socks. Can you get me socks like that?" I floated through the apartment like the pill fairy, microwaving Four Cheese Hot Pockets and tomato soup. Her appetite emerged. I fed her vanilla ice cream and apple pie. I was happy because she seemed happier. She began to explore the apartment. She sat in the pink rocking chair. She hadn't sat there in a long time. She didn't rock at first. One evening, she just sat there. The walls were bare and white except for one painting above the empty fireplace. It was a painting by Mark Rothko. She began to rock a little. I was sitting on the couch. We both stared at the painting.

Back in New Haven, next to Yorkside, there was a little gallery, and this painting was hanging in the window. Ilana once told me she liked it. So, for her birthday in October, I had it framed. Then I made reservations at The Hot Tomato. I asked the manager if he could help me out. It was a surprise, I said, for my girlfriend. When we arrived that evening, I made Ilana close her eyes. I held her hand as we walked up the wooden stairs to our little table by the window overlooking Chapel Street. The table had white, linen cloth and heavy silverware, and there was a single candle burning. I gently sat her down.

"Can I look?"

"Not yet."

I sat. Ilana was wearing this pretty pink dress, and her black hair was down, the way I liked it. I admired her beauty for a moment. Waiting. Eyes closed. There were no other customers. We had the floor to ourselves. I adjusted my tie and saw that two young waitresses were setting the rest of the tables, watching, waiting for Ilana to open her eyes. "OK," I said. "Open." At first, all she saw was me smiling at her. Then she saw the painting. It looked huge sitting on the table, leaning against the wall. The dim lighting and single candle illuminated the painting in a way I did not expect. We both looked at it, as Ilana grabbed for my hands, squeezing them. "I love it. I love you," she said, her skin glowing by the candlelight. I thought she looked like a Rothko painting, too.

"I love you, too," I said. Then I said, "What do you like about it? The painting?"

Ilana looked at it, a great wash of red and orange all swirled together.

"It looks like a sunrise and a sunset at the same time. It looks like where we are going."

Now Ilana had stopped rocking in the pink chair. She stood up. She went to the painting and looked closely. She turned to me and opened her mouth to say something. I could feel it coming. I put on my North Face wool hat for comfort. I had something to say, too. Then she closed her mouth and abruptly marched back to the bedroom and closed the door. The next day, she put on a shoe, just one.

"Going out, Ilana?" I asked, with more excitement than I intended.

"No... I don't know." I patted her on the head, kissed her nose, and hid my disappointment in the microwaving of a Turkey and Cheese Hot Pocket. In the evening, I came into the bedroom with the bottle and spoon.

"Ilana, do you know what time it is?"

"Pill time?"

"Yes, pill time for Ilana!" She washed it down with a gulp of water, and we sang "The Pill Song":

THE PILL SONG

Myron: "The pills make us so happy."
Together: "Yes they do. Yes they do."
Myron: "The pills make us so happy!"
Together: "Yes they do! Yes they do!"

"Such a sweet little pill!" I said.

"Like a blue M&M?" she said.

"Yes!"

For a whole week, she slept with one shoe on her foot. In front of the window, she paced back and forth in one wool sock and one shoe. Clop, sock, clop, sock. She sniffed the windowpane and tapped it a few times when a bee flew near. Once she put her finger on the latch, and I thought she might open it. "Good idea, Ilana! Let's get some fresh air." But she quickly withdrew and clopped back to bed while my Hot Pocket rotated in the microwave.

I smiled at Doctor Greenberg. "I think she's improving."

"Any side effects?"

"Yesterday she peed for three minutes straight. I timed it."

15

"Typical. Anything else?"

"She only eats under the kitchen table. But she makes me sit on a chair."

"I see. I've read about this, I think."

"Is it bad?"

"No! My friend, this is a *good* sign."

"Oh."

"We should up her dose to three pills per day," he said, leaning back in his big chair.

"Three? Okay, but I really wish I could get her in to see you."

"See me, see you—what is the difference, really?"

"I don't know, but it might help. I think she's better, but she still won't leave the apartment."

"Do you remember when you were a little boy, and you were at the top of the playground slide, and you were afraid to go down?"

"No."

"You were up there and just terrified. And then what happened?"

"I slid down?"

"No! My friend, you were pushed."

"I don't remember that."

"It happens to everyone. 'Push Theory' is one of my favorites! It says that no matter what, when in crisis, there is always a *push*, a *force*. It could be someone in your life. It could be you that pushes yourself. Where do you think we get the expression 'push comes to shove'?"

"But—" He stood up, gave me another bottle, and turned me toward the door.

"But I have a few more questions."

"Ah, the world is full of questions, and sometimes the answers do not come until days or years later."

"But—"

"Goodbye, my friend!" he said, holding my elbow and showing me the door.

I rode the bus once again, clutching the unmarked pill bottle in my left hand, whispering, "I love you... I love you... I love you..." Then I put my journal in my lap and wrote, *I'll never leave you; I have to leave you; I'll never leave; I have to leave; I'll never leave...* When I got home, she was under the kitchen table in her pajamas, with one shoe on her foot, eating Honey Nut Cheerios.

"Hello, Ilana," I said.

"Do you love me?" she asked with milk in her mouth.

"Of course!"

"Where were you?"

"I saw Dr. Greenberg. Baby, come out from under the table."

"No."

"I thought you might like to meet him someday. It might be nice for you."

"No."

"He's a nice man. He's fat and jolly!"

"He will hurt me."

"Hush! Ilana, don't be silly." She slurped her milk. Then she stuck out the cereal bowl, and I took it and put it in the sink. "Ilana?" I said, running water into the bowl. "I think... I think you have to see the doctor."

"Why?"

"It would help you."

"No! Leave me alone."

"I thought you never wanted me to leave you," I said.

"Don't leave me. You can't ever leave me," she said.

"I won't, Ilana."

"I hate the doctor!"

"I know, Baby."

"I *hate* him!"

"I know," I said, the water spilling over the bowl. "I know. I know. I know."

A week passed. She stopped wearing her shoe. She declared the window evil. She lay in bed all day and sat under the kitchen table at night. I begged her to come to bed.

She said, "If you love me, you'll come under here." I dragged a blanket and pillow underneath the table and lay next to her. I whispered in her ear, "You warm enough? Shh, Ilana it's OK. Shh, Baby it's OK" until she finally slept. From beneath the kitchen table,

17

through the windowpanes, I watched the sun fill the apartment with jail cells of weird Monday morning light. My eyes were wet and bleary from holding her all night. Telling her "Shh. It's OK. It's all OK." Phone messages piled up like unpaid bills: "Final notice." "Where are you?" "I don't want to fire you, but…" "Please call home." "Your mother is taking Xanax now…" "Your sister said she is driving down if you don't call." "Dude, it's me. Where are you?" "Final notice." "Pay your bill." "Pay your loan." "This is your father. Your mother is crushing her Xanax into her coffee. Please call us." "This is your mother. I'm crying." I tapped three pills into the spoon every day. They did not seem to work. I gave her four then five. She began to hallucinate.

"There's a rat in the closet!"

"There's no rat. Ilana, hush," I said, and patted her sweaty forehead with a damp cloth.

"There's a rat in the closet!"

"Shh. Little baby. I'm making an appointment for you tomorrow. You're going to see the doctor like a big girl."

"No!"

"Yes!"

"No!"

"Please!"

"Fuck you!" I fell into the pink rocking chair and began to cry. Never. Never once had she sworn at me. "Please, Ilana. Please, please. You have to! For me!" I wiped my eyes with my palms.

"I hate you!"

"No, Ilana." I cried hard. "Ilana, please."

"I'm going to fucking die! Kill the rat, or I'll kill myself!"

"Ilana—"

"Fuck you! Leave me alone! No more pills!"

"Please, I—" Suddenly, she lunged at me. We toppled over, the rocking chair splintering into sharp pieces. Then she leapt to her feet and began doing sprints down the hall and back like a thoroughbred, screaming, "NoNoNo!" She ran back and forth for twenty minutes while I sat on the floor with wet eyes, surrounded by pink shards. Finally, she exhausted herself and fell asleep under the kitchen table.

I tiptoed to the door, lightly twisted the knob, and slipped outside to a pay phone. I left a frantic message for Doctor Greenberg. When I got back inside the apartment, Ilana was standing at the door, waiting for me. "Where the *fuck* were you?" she said and reached for me.

I collapsed to the floor, crying like a little boy, pills spilling from my shirt pocket like candy on the floor. I grabbed at them, popping them into my mouth. I tried to swallow, but I was crying too hard, and they choked out. I looked up. Tears bubbled out of her eyes like two boiling pots. Ilana took a step back. She sat down on the bed. I crawled to her, placing my head between her feet like a dog.

I looked up into her eyes. I opened my mouth to say, "I love you. I'm leaving," but her eyes shot each word like skeet. *Bang! Bang! Bang! Bangbang!* They exploded and fell to the floor. I collected the pieces and put them on a porcelain dish on the nightstand. She shoved the dish to the floor, and it shattered. I vacuumed. She ran to the living room, seized a pink shard, and slashed the vacuum bag, and we both choked on the particles of dust and love.

I crawled on my belly to the answering machine. Forty-one messages unread. "Hi, it's me again, hope everything is OK." "It's Mom, please call me back." "Dude, it's George, where are you?" "It's your father. Your mother is drinking heavily. Call back, or I'm calling the police." "This is the police…" "This is Cathy Jones calling about your application to graduate school at…" I reached for the stop button, but I was too late.

"Did you fucking apply to *graduate* school?" she said, standing over me. She swooped down like an eagle over a lake and ripped the cord out of the wall. I slid off the couch like a thin sheet and lay on the ground. Suddenly, she lay on top of me, nibbling my lower lip. "I love you," she said.

"What?" I said, choking on a cry.

"I love you."

"I love you, too," I said, and my eyes liquefied.

"How do I know?" she said, licking my nose, kissing my wet eyes. I cried. She smothered me like an old afghan, full of holes but warm and familiar. On the hard wood we tangled, sheet and afghan, wet lips, wet eyes. "I love you so much," I said. "And you love me." I cried like a wife whose husband had emerged from a collapsed mine, sirens blaring, ambulance ready, rescue workers, journalists, and neighbors hooting, crying, and clapping. "The girl from New Haven," I said, "the girl I first met in New Haven!"

"It's me," she said, and smiled. I laughed. Tears zigzagged down my cheeks like confused children at play in a landmine field. Suddenly, the doorbell buzzed like a wasp. "Open up! It's Doctor Greenberg!"

"Bastard!" she cried, leaping to her feet. She opened the door and stabbed him in the belly with a pink, wooden dagger. The doctor hit the wall, opened his mouth, and vomited pills. Ilana jumped down three steps at a time, crashed like symbols into the sunlight, and galloped like a horse with a broken leg, neighing at cars. I ran after her, crying, screaming like a nurse. Dr. Greenberg stumbled after us, "Say what needs to be said!" he hollered. I looked back as he collapsed, holding his belly, as little blue pills retched from his mouth like Pez.

***

Ilana jumped the curb and loped across 15th Street. A red Subaru Forester smashed its horn and skidded on its tires. A bike messenger swerved and clipped her shoulder, but still she ran on. A dozen vehicles honked like a flock of enraged geese. People stopped and stared. A chubby woman wearing black skinny jeans picked up her Chihuahua and held it close, whispering in its ear. The little dog's bulging eyes stared at me in horror. A slender little man in a suit and blue tie, holding a long black umbrella, yelled, "Do you need help?" The sun winked out. From every direction, rain clouds gathered like gray missiles. They met above us and exploded into a water bomb. Big, meaty drops of rain like little boxing gloves punched the pavement, the hoods of the cars, and between the slots of the bike messenger's aerodynamic helmet.

Ilana made it to the other side of the street. I chased after her, apologizing to everyone. The bike messenger gave me the finger. The people in their cars all pushed down their horns and held them so that the street sounded like one, deep organ blast in a cathedral, raining on the inside.

I ran to her, yelling "Ilana!" Dr. Greenberg followed, holding his belly, yelling "Myron!" I ran past the man with the blue tie, his umbrella now up.

"Do you need help?" he asked again as I rushed past. I didn't answer, but I wanted to say, "Yes! Please!" Why was I always so afraid to ask for help? Why did I always listen to the wrong people? There are so many smart people in this world, and there are so many stupid people. The one thing they have in common is that they all want to give you advice. Why couldn't I figure out the bad from good? What was wrong with me?

Ilana turned hard left down P Street and disappeared. The rain beat the top of my head. The wind snapped like snakes on Medusa's head. When I turned the corner, Ilana was gone. My face was wet. My armpits were sweaty. My shoes were soaked. I slowed to a panicked walk. Stone and brick apartments lined both sides of the street. I looked inside a window and saw a young couple hugging. Cars and trucks now waited at a red light. Their windshield wipers on high, all moving in unison like giant fingers wagging at me, telling me I was doing something wrong, that I had failed us both. My whole life I had felt guilty, and now the guilt detonated inside me, its lifelong fuse finally reaching the dynamite. I saw an alley and heard something rustle. Overwhelmed, I turned and staggered in.

"Ilana?" I said, more quietly. My voice shook with guilt and shame and love and fear. Overwhelmed, I collapsed and began to sob, rain and sweat and tears all drizzling down my cheeks. I cried for Ilana. I cried for my mother and father. I cried out for help. "I'm sorry!" I yelled into the cold rain. And what was I sorry for? For every mistake I had ever made. For moving to D.C. If we hadn't moved here, none of this would have happened. We should have stayed in New Haven where my family was close. I could have gotten Ilana help, real help. We could have rescued a Black Lab puppy and saved up for a little one-bedroom house and we would have danced across an oak floor in our socks with a full moon glowing through a big French window. "I'm sorry," I said again, but the rain ate my words like a million wet mouths.

How did we get here? I wondered. How did we become so isolated? I scuttled like a beetle up to the wall of the alley between two black trash bags—water running down them in little zigzags. Why couldn't I let go of all this fear and pain? Why are all my friends' lives so much easier? I wanted my mommy. I wanted my daddy. I wanted to see my sister. I *needed* to warm myself by their stove-like, fiery love for me, for us. I wanted Ilana back, the girl from New Haven. We had to get back, somehow. Cars made slicking noises out on P Street. A young couple sharing an umbrella walked past the alley. They stopped and looked at me.

"Are you OK?" the man said.

"No," I said, in a voice so quiet that God Himself could not hear.

The man made a movement towards me, but the girl touched his arm, and he held back, and they moved on.

The rain fell on my head. It wriggled like tadpoles down my neck and burrowed into my socks and shoes. My right hand touched something sharp. I looked down and saw a broken beer bottle. Little green shards gleamed in the rain, and for the first time in my life, I thought about it.

***

I felt something in my back-left pocket. It was my journal. I quickly grabbed it. Luckily it was dry, even though my jeans were heavy and wet. I pressed myself deeper against the wall where I was somewhat sheltered, the rain now tapping down only on my knees and feet. I opened to the last entry and saw that I had written "THINGS I AM GRATEFUL FOR GO HERE." I remembered that, in the online forum about Dr. Greenberg, someone had mentioned that a "gratitude journal" had helped them to climb out of their hole. Something about writing down everything you were grateful for, even if you feel like you have nothing good in your life. I looked at the green shards with a longing that scared me. I imagined how quickly I could do it. I imagined my blood mingling with the rain and emptying into a sewer grate in the alley. I picked one up. It was thin and sharp. It had a point. I put it to my wrist and held it there, just for a second. I thought about my mom and dad. I thought about my sister. I imagined them crying over small granite tombstone. I thought about Ilana. My eyes watered, wet and bleary. Something small but fierce inside said *no*. I dropped the shard. I fished out a pen, squished up my knees to balance my journal, and I began to write.

MYRON'S GRATITUDE JOURNAL

Things I am grateful for—even though I feel I am dying:

- I am… I am grateful for… my mom.
- I am grateful for my dad.
- I am grateful for my sister.
- I am grateful for ~~Hana~~ Ilana.
- I am grateful for the breath in my lungs.
- The rain in my socks.
- My friend George.
- I am grateful for the fact that I'm still alive.
- I breathe air all day long. I can still do that.
- I am not dead, yet.
- I have lots of work yet to do.
- I am a good person.
- Ilana is a… Ilana is a great person.
- I have a future. With Ilana. Somewhere.
- I still have years to go and contribute meaningfully to this world.
- ~~I~~ WE can go anywhere we want on earth.
- We are not alone.
- I am not alone.
- I'm lucky people love me despite the wicked things closing in.
- We will survive this darkness.
- I am very good at sex. I just am. I can't forget that.
- I am applying to grad school. Maybe I'll get in. I will get in.
- We will not die in D.C.
- We are valuable.
- We are good.
- The sun came up today, somewhere.
- I am better than this place.
- I will not live in fear of monsters.

- I will not walk on eggshells or landmines.
- I will walk with purpose and strength.
- I will speak with love and compassion.
- No amount of water can wink out my fire.
- No darkness can ink out my light.
- I will not be crushed by anyone.
- I am un-crushable.
- I am a bouncy ball.
- I will be a lighthouse.
- I *am* a lighthouse.
- I was *meant* to be a lighthouse.
- I radiate light.
- I am a beacon.
- No matter how many waves like whips crack upon my skin, I am always a light, radiating outwards even as I drown. I am the lighthouse and the little boat in the storm. I will follow myself to shore.
- There is no extinguisher to put out the fire that burns inside me. For what can stop an inside fire?
- There is no pain that can cover me, for I am a mountain.
- There is no lack of compassion that I cannot withstand.
- My compassion is enough for us both.
- There is no lack of energy in my environment, for my internal energy needs no batteries or electricity—only the air I breathe.
- I imagine bolts of blue energy flashing out of my hands, illuminating the dark sky like upside down lightning.
- I am always light.
- I am spark.
- I am flame.
- I am what I was meant to be—even if I don't feel sometimes that I have gotten there yet.
- My wet feet are in my socks. My wet socks are in my shoes. My wet shoes are on the pavement. I am here.
- My path has always been under me.
- I live in D.C., and I hate it, but I love everyone—even those who are against me us.

- Darkness was made for light.
- No matter where I end up, I will be there.
- The love in my heart has always been enough.
- An eyedropper of kindness is all I ask.
- Surely you can squeeze out that much for me—or anyone?
- I liquefy compassion.
- I put it on a spoon.
- I gulp.
- I want to go home. No, I want us to go home, back to New Haven.
- Maybe I can get us home?
- I *will* get us home.
- Ilana feels like an electric blanket on high, in the winter, in New Haven.
- Even now, Ilana's teenage-tight ass gives me a hard on.
- Rain outside. Rain in our apartment. Rain in this alley. Rain in my eyes. No matter…
- In my head, we are going home. But I have already always been home.
- Home is just good energy.
- I must get us back to New Haven.
- I *will* get us back.
- I try to make everyone around me feel safe.
- What else is there to do?
- I imagine a stranger reading this someday.
- Whoever you are, you are loved.
- If you are sad or angry or suicidal, do this.
- Turn off your poison phone.
- Find the nearest person and ask them.
- "How can I help?"
- There is no such thing as a small act of kindness.
- For all kindness is a galaxy.
- I have not smiled in seven months.
- I must get back to the Old Myron, which will be the New Myron.
- I must let go.
- I will let go.
- I *am* letting go…

- I let go. And I stay.
- At the same time.
- I feel an itch.
- I feel it but do not scratch.
- I simply *feel* it.
- And let it go.
- What is your itch?
- Can you not scratch?
- The trick is to learn to become comfortable with un-comfortableness.
- My winter breath is visible in the rain.
- I love my breath, for wherever I go, there it is.
- My fire is not out. Embers smolder, waiting…
- I just need a log and a little breath.
- The log is in my mind. It's my decision to ignite myself. Yours, too.
- It's hard for me, right now. If it's hard for you, too, just know I love you.
- I haven't meditated in three years. When I did, I would see stars parting to my left and right as I travelled in hyperspace. Then the stars would fade. There was just *now*. Black and infinite, moving and not moving at the same time.
- A little fly just landed on my left cheek. I will not touch it. I sit with it. The fly and I are here, right now, floating together in the present like a space buoy bobbing in an ocean made of light.
- I miss a lot of people. I miss Ilana, even when I'm kissing her.
- But I'm thankful for any moment I have shared with her. When she laughs, I feel like I'm in a hot shower. Each drop of water is a smile. My naked body is covered in smiles.
- I am grateful that my mom hates to see me suffer.
- I forgive her for any mistake she ever made as a parent.
- I forgive my father for any mistake he made as a parent. They did their best, and their best was like an LED flashlight when I was dark, an umbrella when it rained, a hot stove in the winter. Their love has always been enough. I just didn't see it, for I was looking at the wrong screen. Hitting rewind and rewind and rewind on all the bad stuff. I now take out the DVD of Anger. And put in the DVD of Love and let it play and feel gratitude. It's my decision what to watch.

- I am grateful for the wet and cold I feel right now. Because I know that soon I will be warm again.
- I am grateful for my sister who sent me a message two days ago saying that she was proud of me and that "This darkness will pass into light."
- I am grateful for my friend Jacob who told me it will be Ok.
- I am grateful for my friend George who told me it will be Ok.
- I am grateful for my friend Frank who told me it will be Ok.
- I am grateful for my father who hugged me one morning and said, "I love you." Then hugged me again after cleaning the snow from his Honda and said, "I love you." What more can I need? I have it all.
- I am grateful because the sun is bright. It's always there, even at night.
- I am grateful for the mug of ginger tea I will drink with Ilana in New Haven when we go back to the Book Trader Cafe.
- I am grateful that I can still doggy paddle back to shore.
- I am grateful for another day, another hour, another moment to… begin again.
- I am grateful for another breath in my lungs. One breath. Two. Three. Four…
- I am grateful knowing that soon this pain will be over.
- I am grateful because I know what I need to do, as do you. You have always known.
- I am grateful for the love that radiates out of my mother and father's collective heart. It burns like a bonfire, and for too long I have stayed inside while they were out there, beckoning me, "warm yourself by our light." One day they won't be there, and I must soak up their warmth and store it for the rest of my life.
- I am grateful that someday I WE will get a dog.
- Is the past an anchor around my neck? A chain holding down my rocket ship? I must get us back to New Haven and find out…
- I am grateful knowing that someday I will smile again.
- I must find Old Myron, and laugh and be the Me that was joyous and funny and made others laugh. My gifts are melting. I have not met my potential. I will, in grad school. I will someday meet my potential and shake his hand and hug him and laugh! And we will

merge like shadow and light and float in the sky like a leaf, not worried about the direction of the wind. Wind will come and go. We/me will simply float, like a buoy in an ocean of us.

- The number of times I've said thank you is equal to the number of times I've said I'm sorry. Why?
- I'm so sorry, Ilana, for wasting years walking backwards in the right direction.
- But I am still here now.
- Still here because, wherever I go, there I am.
- Wherever I go, I imagine roots growing from the bottom of my feet. Feet like roots for you and I. I am an oak tree. Even if I'm crying in the rain, in an alley, in D.C., lonely and scared and depressed, I cry like an oak.
- I am grateful for this darkness, for soon it will be light.

I snapped my journal shut. From inside the garbage bag next to me, I fished out a small plastic bag from CVS. Carefully I wrapped my journal in it and tucked it into my pocket. The rain turned to drizzle. I stood up. I wiped my eyes with my wet sleeve. I looked at the green shards again and said *No*.

Just then, I heard Dr. Greenberg stagger into the alley.

"Myron!" he bellowed, "Take these! Say what you need to say. Take these!"

He held forth his right hand, filled with little blue pills. I hopped to my feet and bolted down the alley. Dr. Greenberg staggered onwards, still holding his bleeding stomach. I zigzagged around deep puddles. From behind a garbage bag, a soaking rat dove at me. I leapt over it in a dead sprint, not looking back.

I made it to the other end of the alley. Cars and trucks swished over the slick streets.

"Ilana!"

I waited.

I listened for seven breaths.

I heard a little rustling sound like a mouse in a paper bag and found her lying on a flattened cardboard box. There was blue vomit next to her mouth. Her black hair was wet and matted to her cheeks. I picked her up and put her arm over my shoulder. She eked out a little,

"No." I didn't say anything but kept us moving. From the corner of my eye, I saw Dr. Greenberg limping down the alley, wet, bleeding, pleading with me to take more little blue pills.

The rain shut off as if someone had turned a faucet. The sidewalk bristled with women in stylish rain boots and men in trench coats. They folded and closed dripping umbrellas and looked at us like homeless, troubled kids. A little boy holding his mother's hand pointed at us and laughed. She pulled him close and wedged herself between the child and us. We struggled forward, slowly, parting a sea of urban professionals. They moved to the left and right, just like the stars that used to part when I meditated. Up ahead, I saw the sign I wanted: Enterprise Car Rentals.

I opened the door, and a cheerful bell rang as if we were normal customers. Gently, I lowered Ilana onto a cushioned seat and went to the counter. "I need a car," I said, wet and crazed, pulling out my saturated wallet. Behind the counter, a young woman wearing a navy-blue cardigan pushed up her hipster glasses and looked at Ilana as if I had spilled a cup of liquid sadness on her clean waiting area. "Please," I said. She looked at me, then looked around as seeking help. "Please," I said, and slid my debit card across the white counter. I had exactly $729 in my account. *Should be enough*, I thought, *always just enough, like a demented Tarzan swinging from a vine, hoping the next will be there to catch.*

After speaking with her manager, the woman gave me the keys to a green Kia Soul. She hugged her arms tightly around herself as I signed the paperwork. I lifted Ilana from her seat—transferring her as if she were a psych-ward patient needing assistance getting out of a wheelchair—and dragged her outside to the lot. I found the car, poured her in, and clicked her seatbelt into place. I ran to the other side and got in. Ilana mumbled something, but I couldn't understand. I turned on the car and the windshield wipers to push away the last of the rain. As I began to pull out, Dr. Greenberg suddenly pounded on the window. He mushed his body to the driver's side, smearing it with belly blood.

"Myron! You found her! Take these! Say what you need to say!"

I honked the horn.

"Go away! We don't need you!"

Something fiercely protective came over me, and I considered backing up and slamming into him. I looked at Ilana. She seemed to be melting, getting smaller and smaller. I turned on the heat full blast and swiveled all the vents towards her.

"Don't worry," I said, "everything is going to be OK. Alright?"

Dr. Greenberg wailed and smeared. I blasted the horn.

"Go the fuck away!" I turned to Ilana.

"Wait. Listen. Everything *is* Ok. We *are* OK."

I found the exit, driving slowly so that I did not hit any cars, which gave Dr. Greenberg a chance to follow us. Cars and trucks whooshed by on the slick road. None of them seemed to care about us. I had to wait for an opening. Dr. Greenberg came to us in a final attempt. He held out his hand, filled with little blue pills. Ilana groaned as if she could feel them near, like blue magnets pulling at her blood. Dr. Greenberg pounded the window with his other palm. "Take these. You will need them!" A little break in the traffic. I slammed on the gas and spun the tires, and we flew into the street. Dr. Greenberg fell to the pavement. I adjusted the rearview mirror, and I saw him on his knees, his great stomach covered in blood, as he opened his mouth and let the little blue pills roll down his throat like quarters being fed into a slot machine.

I didn't have my phone or a map. But we were close to the highway. I followed signs and finally found the big green one I was looking for. I pulled onto the ramp for 95 North. New Haven. Home.

It was growing darker and darker. The highway lamps glowed orange-red. I finally realized my lights were not on and flipped the lever. I sped up to sixty-five, seventy-one, seventy-four. The little Kia shook. Ilana mumbled something.

"What was that baby?

"No," she said.

"Guess where we're going? New Haven! We're going home, baby."

"No," she said, in a voice that was distant as the moon. Suddenly, she rolled down the window and retched a bluish substance that streaked the side of car. Blood on one side. Blue on the other.

Her wet hair thrashed in the wind as she heaved. I eased off the gas. When she finished, I pushed the button to roll up her window then accelerated. Sixty-eight, seventy-nine. Eighty-one...

"It's OK, baby," I said, and put my hand on her knee. She didn't even wipe her mouth as she melted again. Was she fading? Purging?

"Baby, do you know where we are going? New Haven. Home," I said, patting her knee.

"It won't work," she said in a small voice like a woman who had just been slapped in the face. I wanted her to throw up again and again and again. The headlights of the cars looked like a thousand little beacons telling me *Yes! Yes! Go faster!*

"New Haven, baby. Remember?"

Very calmly she said, "It won't work."

My voice slipped a notch. "Yes, baby. It will."

"No, it won't." My hands trembled. I touched the journal in my pocket. *Soon it will be light.* I knuckled the shaky steering wheel and pressed the gas pedal with my wet shoe. It was dark now, and Ilana said something I couldn't hear then fell asleep, her head leaning against the window.

I squeezed the wheel like a talisman. Eighty-two, Eighty-three... Tires slicked. Wind pushed the little car like a bully. Beacons everywhere. The smell of rain and highway pavement cleansed my nostrils, cleared my mind. *It's gonna work*, I thought, *New Haven.* I listened to the quiet sound of Ilana breathing as I drove as fast as I could, the two of us in our little Soul, crying north.

MISTAKE

It was a beautiful old brownstone built in 1897. It was on Second Street right in downtown Troy—my new home. The brownstone had four stories. The apartments in the front had big windows that let in the August light. They had little balconies surrounded by wrought-iron railing. Some tenants had colorful flowers or nice green plants out there. The front doors were heavy, thick wood. It took a little *oomph* to open them. Inside, the place was all wood floors and oak wainscoting. Big oil paintings hung on the walls. There was a leather couch and our mailboxes. The staircase looked like it had taken a master carpenter years to engrave elaborate designs and etch little runes into the railing. This was my new apartment building, but I didn't live in the front. I lived in the back. My fat landlord, Martin, said it used to be a servant's quarters. He called it a "one bedroom," but that's only because it fit *a* bed in its *one* room.

"This isn't what the ad said," I told him, waving a printout from Craigslist. The ad had a picture of the front of the building and interiors from the nicer apartments. Fat Martin put his hands in his pockets and shrugged his shoulders as if to say, *Yeah, you got me.* I sighed and took the place. It was cheap. I was broke. My $1,400-per-month PhD stipend hadn't kicked in yet.

The day I moved in, I parked my rented van on the sidewalk. I opened the back double-doors and pulled out the first box. In black permanent marker, I had written "Ilana" in a scribbly, shaky hand. I kind of got lost for a minute thinking about her, so I didn't see Fat Martin on the sidewalk. He was wearing a black helmet with a GoPro camera strapped on top. He had a clipboard in his hands.

"Is that recording?" I asked. Fat Martin looked down at his clipboard. He shrugged his shoulders.

"It's for legal purposes. New tenants and whatnot. I like to keep a record. It's in the lease."

"What? Where?" I hadn't read the lease at all. I'm a moron about stuff like that. I know I *should* read it carefully, but little details like that scare me. I can't seem to concentrate on them. I just kind of assume everything will be OK. That good will win out over evil. That reasonable people will be nice to me. I *feel* my way through the world, eyes half closed, living in a dream bubble. I paint pictures in my head, pictures of the future I am completely positive might possibly happen, as long as I just keep painting. I live in a daydream, even at night. I live in a sequence dream, an if-then-statement life. I always imagine that *if* this thing just happens, or *if* I can just get past this *one* problem *then* everything will magically be all right. I was scared of the present, so I focused on the future until the present faded into the past. Then I could ruminate about it, forever. Such is the anxious life. I once read in a book by this Buddhist nun, Pema Chödrön who said that when life gets scary, when things get uncomfortable, we have two options. We can wake up or shutdown. We can awaken to the moment, to the pain and fear and learn to be comfortable with uncomfortable things. Or we can shutdown, take a nap, take a pill, watch reality TV, drink beer, smoke cigarettes. Hell, we can even go to the gym. We can do anything to distract ourselves from what is really happening. When I read that, I realized that I was a shutdowner and that I always would be. Waking up is hard and scary, so I figured I would just get good at being in denial. I don't think that's what Pema had in mind, but that's the best I could do back then.

"It's at the bottom of the lease. In parenthesis," Fat Martin said.

To get to my apartment, I had to walk down a long alley made of brick. The door opened to a little vestibule containing my door and stairs leading to another apartment. My place had only one window, which faced the alley. From that window, I got one little dagger of sunlight stabbing into the place. It was dark all the time except for that yellow Lightsaber of sun. I sort of liked it. It was my Hobbit hole, except not as nice. A Hobbit would not have lived there. But the place made sense to me. I lived most of my life in the dark back then, so this was the perfect place. My tiny, dark, yet cozy apartment was in perfect harmony with my anxious mind. Especially after the whole thing with Ilana. My mom wanted me to get a place with some light. Maybe she was right, but I don't think I could have dealt with that. For most of my adult life, the sun had been my mortal enemy. I preferred New England gloom over sunshine.

I was alone and terrified about starting my PhD, but at least that nervousness felt comfortable. For a little while, there was no one else to worry about. I was finally free to be the nervous little guy that I was destined to be.

That August, I had decided I was going to smoke a lot of cigarettes and take a lot of Xanax. I was in transition. Eight months earlier, Ilana and I had exploded in a mushroom cloud of love and fear, and now I had one month before classes began. My mind ping-ponged between the past and the future. *Thwack!* I would ruminate about Ilana then *thwack!* I'd be paddled forward, terrified about things that haven't even happened yet. Excitement and anxiety swished in my blood like vodka and tomato juice. The first few days, I was so nervous that my skin broke out in red, itchy bumps. The only way to soothe myself was to take a cold shower. Then I'd put on my New Haven t-shirt and brown North Face wool hat, pop a Xanax (.5 MG), and write in my journal while smoking a Marlboro Light. Smoking was a new habit. After the War of D.C., I needed *something*. I didn't know what. A hobby? Some people collect stamps, or do yoga, so I figured I would smoke, a lot.

Sometimes I went outside. Troy was schizophrenic. One street gave you lovely Victorian architecture, tree-lined cobblestone sidewalks, and cafes with little wrought-iron tables outside. The next street was filled with empty storefronts, broken windows, and Troylits lingering like weird Sunday shadows. That's what the RPI kids called the locals. They were "Troylits" because they considered Troy the toilet bowl of upstate New York. Much later, I found out that a dirty political scheme allowed New York City to bus a lot of their crazies up to Troy where they had public housing set up. They did this one, crazy spoonful at a time as if the city were a doctor telling Troy to "open wide." Reluctantly, at first, Troy would swallow its spoonful as if each person were a little crazy pill. And over the years, Troy became a once-beautiful city filled with insane people. Troy was like a wealthy, elegant older woman who got dementia and was left to wither in a nursing home. None of her kids coming to visit.

At the edge of town was The Approach, an ancient set of marble stairs that wound up a steep, grassy hill. At the top of the hill, overlooking all this beautiful weirdness was Rensselaer Polytechnic Institute, the country's oldest technological institute, which sneered at Troy with mistrust the way rich people in the suburbs peek through their blinds when a slow-moving van drives through the neighborhood.

I was starting to regret my life decisions. I was now a first-year PhD student in Applied General Studies. RPI was the only place I got in. Had I made a mistake going to grad school? Should I have just moved home? Gotten a real job like my friends? They all had kids, wives, homes. They were unhappy but stable. I was unhappy *and* unstable. I wasn't sure what to think, but I knew I had made a mistake when Samuel took off his shorts.

For a few weeks, I was sort-of happy in my quiet little apartment. I had almost no sunlight, no Internet, and no TV. I locked myself inside, read fantasy novels, smoked Marb Lights, and explored deep into the dusty archives of my jerk-off files. It's my own perverted Instagram that lives in my mind, filled with images of all the girls that unwittingly help me jerk off. There isn't Gwyneth Paltrow or Penelope Cruz in these files because I can't *imagine* a situation in which famous, beautiful women would want me. No, these images are of the cute brunette cashier at Target, the thirty-nine-year-old MILF on OkCupid showing off her little bikini body because she needs to prove that she's still got it, the petite indie snob with green hair who works at the artsy, vegan cafe, who's a *total* bitch, but she's hot, so she gets away with it. These files go as far back as high school, where images of pink cheerleader asses are frozen in time. The files even extend into the future, where I imagine that legalized prostitution and a blowjob is merely an iPhone tap away. My files are rather extensive, more like the National Archives. I was dusting them off, swiping left through images, naked on my bed when suddenly there was a knock-knock-knock on the door.

Frustrated, I quickly wrapped up in a towel and opened the door. Standing in front of me and grinning like a maniac was Samuel. He was forty-eight with a shaved head. He had no shirt. For his age, he was in good shape. His stomach was flat, his biceps toned and sinewy. He was wearing very short cutoffs, like Daisy Dukes. He wore white flip-flops. His bare chest was shaved and waxed.

"Myron!" he shouted. I had met Samuel at The Ruck three days before. He said he was the janitor there, and I felt bad for him. He said he was living from couch to couch and sometimes sleeping in the basement with the mop, broom, and chemicals.

I told him Fat Martin had a vacant apartment and that he worked out deals sometimes. I figured Samuel could keep the place clean, shovel the snow, and take out the trash. Sure enough, my plan worked. Now Samuel was my neighbor, living upstairs, and I had never seen him outside of his janitor clothes: old jeans, blue Carhartt sweatshirt, and a carabineer with a clanking of keys. Now he was half-naked and outside my door. It was eleven in the morning, and he smelled like beer. "Umm, hi," I said. He noticed the towel.

"Are you naked?" he asked.

"Umm…I was just in the shower."

"You're completely dry," he said, grinning.

"Well, I—"

"You want me to jump in with you?"

"What?" I said, tightening my towel. He took a step closer. I took a step back.

"You heard me." I held my towel with both hands.

"Joking! I'm just joking! OK, Myron, gotta go." He smirked and left, and I closed the door. Suddenly, his bald head appeared at my window. "Myron. Hey, Myron! I was just joking. I'm not gay. I think about it sometimes, but I'm not gay." I walked over, shut the window, locked it, and put on a pair of black sweatpants, my New Haven t-shirt, and my brown North Face wool hat.

For two weeks, Samuel ran up and down the stairs in his Daisy Dukes. He owned no furniture except a cot. I had no idea what he was doing, but he was always on the move. I never saw him with a shirt. He tanned in the backyard in his cutoffs. Once, I saw him carry a huge aluminum ladder on his shoulder—wearing his Daisy Dukes and flip-flops—and disappear around the back of the building. He drank every day, starting around ten o'clock. I never saw him eat. I never really saw him work. He asked for money. I gave him twenty bucks, and he came back with a six-pack and no change. When he greeted me, he always put his hand on my shoulder, sometimes both. Whenever I heard him go upstairs and close his door, he was quiet. Too quiet. He never played loud music. He never had parties. The silence terrified me.

He would drink at The Ruck until dawn. One morning, I was about to go for coffee at Starbucks when I heard the alley door open and close. I heard footsteps in the vestibule. This time I looked out of my peephole first. Samuel was swaying drunkenly. He stripped off his shirt. Then he unzipped his Daisy Dukes and took out his thingy. He stood there for a moment. Arms akimbo. His thingy was drunk, too. It was swaying. He held his hand out to knock on my door. But he hesitated. They both swayed. He grinned. Then he shook his head and walked upstairs in his flip-flops. I waited a few minutes then quietly left and didn't come back all day.

Samuel began knocking on my door in the morning. "Hello! Have a good day!" Then at noon, "Eat a good lunch!" Then at ten o'clock at night, he'd bang on the window, and give me a thumbs-up, and a window-muffled, "Myron!" He asked me if I had any weed. He asked me where he could find ecstasy. He banged on my door at midnight to ask if I had a pillow that he could borrow. "Not a soft one. I like them nice and firm," he said and grinned.

Things got worse. On a Friday night, I came home to find the alleyway front door open and Samuel in his tiny shorts, halfway up the stairs shouting at what he *said* was a man in his apartment. The second night, he was shouting again. When I opened my door, Samuel turned and barked at me, "Don't call the cops! I swear to God, don't call the cops!" He kicked the wall with his flip-flop, and I shut the door and locked it. The next morning, Samuel knocked on my door to tell me not to worry. Everything was fine. "How about that shower," he said and grinned, putting a hand on each of my shoulders. I imagined that an image of me was stored in *his* jerk-off files.

"Is everything OK?" I said, "Like, are you OK?" Samuel grinned. His tan, bald head made a strange contrast against the white walls of the vestibule.

"Oh, sweetie," he said, "Everything's just fine," and he patted me on my brown North Face wool hat then quietly walked upstairs. The next day I called Fat Martin to complain. He showed up wearing his helmet and GoPro.

"You believe you are a very attractive man, don't you?" he asked, staring at his clipboard.

"No! What are you talking about? He's crazy! He drinks every day and never eats! He's a drug addict. He bangs on my door day and night. He threatened me!" Fat Martin tapped his helmet with his knuckle and shook his head side-to-side. "Sorry, can you repeat that?"

"What? I just told you. He's *fuck*ing crazy!"

"How long have you been a homophobe?" Fat Martin asked.

"I'm not a homophobe!" I cried, and slammed the door in his face.

Left alone, I considered entrapment. I could plant drugs, *gay* drugs in his apartment and call the cops. I was pondering how to murder Samuel and get away with it when he banged on my door and asked me to come upstairs. I was afraid to say yes and scared to say no. The previous tenant had left the place a mess, and he wanted to show me how much he had cleaned. When I got up there, he closed the door. He locked the deadbolt. I told him it was very clean, trying to smile and keep him happy. Samuel walked over to the bed. He grinned and pulled down his Daisy Dukes. He was naked. Then he slid his hand underneath the pillow I had given him. He pulled out a large kitchen knife and a roll of duct tape. He grinned at me. I almost thought his thingy was grinning, too. I ran for the door, the lock fumbling in my terrified fingers.

"Myron, sweetie. Are you experiencing *fear*?" he said and laughed.

I got the door open and leapt for the stairs. I tripped and tumbled down, down, down.

I was on my back. I opened my eyes. A screaming pain radiated out of my right leg. Samuel was standing over me, naked, knife in his hand, and Fat Martin was there with his helmet and GoPro.

"Myron. My name is Dr. Samuel Flagson. I'm not really a janitor. I am a professor in the Department of Experimental Gay

Chemistry at RPI. Martin is my research assistant and an old friend."
Fat Martin stopped scribbling notes in his clipboard. He looked at me
and shrugged his shoulders like *yeah, you know.*

Samuel began to tell me about his life. How he grew up just
outside of Dallas, the adopted son of two gay men. His father taught
high school biology and his other father pioneered nude Skype therapy
in Texas. He told me of all the hateful things the kids said to him as a
boy. How they always tried to stick their pencils up his "gay butt" and
called him "Sam Fagson." He told me all about how he spent much of
his adult life in a laboratory, filled with anger, trying to find a solution.
Then 9/11 happened.

"Sorry about all this," Samuel continued, "but lying is the only
way to get an honest reaction from our test subjects." He played with
the edge of the knife. Then he said, "Last year, I was awarded a $10
million grant from the U.S. Department of Defense in conjunction with
Starbucks—it's a PR thing for them, you know. Anyways, the DOD
and Starbucks are hoping to harness the fear of gays and weaponize
it to combat global terrorism. We placed nanosensors all around your
apartment. They're like little sponges. They absorb your gay fear,
which we then squeeze out and turn into a chemical weapon. It's like
gay Anthrax, or what we call Homothrax. Deadly stuff. We are hoping
to use drones to test it out on the Taliban in Afghanistan, as well as
some parts of Dallas and South Troy this semester. And because of
you, we will have a lot more stockpiled. Your fear of gays is off the
charts!"

"I'm *not* a homophobe" I said, clutching my leg, which I was
sure had broken in the fall. "It's not gay fear. It's just fear. I'm afraid
all the time!"

Fat Martin handed me an iPad showing me on my futon wearing
my brown North Face hat with my shirt pushed up and my sweatpants
bunched around only one ankle.

"You taped me?" I said.

"Of course!" said Professor Flagson. "And you know what?
You jerk off a lot. I mean, it's incredible. And you always fall asleep
so peacefully. You look so calm and happy." All I could do was sigh
like and grab at my leg.

"Don't worry. No one will see these videos except for everyone on the research team, a few low-ranking generals at the DOD and, of course, some high-level executives at Starbucks. Maybe a few focus groups, stuff like that. You have performed a great service for your country. Martin will take five percent off your rent next month for any inconvenience. You also get this coupon for one free Grande coffee at any participating Starbucks." He placed the coupon and some documents for me to review and sign next to my busted leg. Fat Martin shrugged his shoulders. Professor Flagson, still naked, stood directly over my head. I looked up at the horrible dangle. With his fingers, he flicked the flat part of the knife's blade.

"You know," he said, "I never thought you hated gay people. I just thought you were a pussy." Fat Martin chuckled then took out some more papers and dropped them next to me, along with a pen. Samuel continued.

"Myron, a few months ago, the President of RPI dissolved your PhD program. It was the last program on earth of its kind. The rest of your cohort, the last to be admitted, has already declined to attend. Unfortunately, we sent your letter to an old address, somewhere in New Haven, I think. Anyways, you showed up, and so, legally, we are forced to teach you and allow you to finish your degree, which is unfortunate." Fat Martin snickered a little, taking more notes. "Of course, now that our experiment is finished, you may quit before classes begin. Would you like that, Myron?" My leg ached, but my head hurt even worse. If what Samuel was saying was true, I could quit and move back to... somewhere. But I thought about Ilana and my plan. I thought about my parents and how I did not want to disappoint them. I thought about the real world and how scary it was. What would I do? Work in a cubicle? Answer phones? Work at a Starbucks? I could never take a job out there, and I had no idea where else to apply. Maybe with this program being dissolved, it would be easier to get through? Maybe I could hide here and be the last, best student they ever had. My head hurt. My leg hurt. I wasn't thinking straight. Then Samuel bent down on his haunches. His powerful thingy was only inches from my forehead. I could smell it.

"Well," Samuel said, "What do you have to say?" He was looking directly down at me, piano-key teeth gleaming.

I wanted to get up, but Samuel showed no sign of moving. I was afraid my head would graze his thingy. Without moving from my back, I reached for the paper and pen. I signed my name. I would be the last student on earth to earn a PhD in Applied General Studies.

"Ha!" he said. "Well, Myron. Now that you have signed your name, there is no going back. I have been assigned as your PhD advisor. Your dissertation committee members, should you get that far, will be Associate Professor Dr. Seattle Freedom and Professor Alexis Smith-Smith. Good luck with grad school, though I doubt you'll get through it!" Fat Martin took the papers and held the door open for Samuel.

Still holding the knife, he walked out the front door humming the RPI fight song, his proud thingy swinging in triumph.

IBABY

When iBaby arrived, my whole world changed. It began six years ago, when two lonely, unmarried engineering professors in the Department of Science and Danger drank a little too much wine and stayed up all night designing a secret machine that would, as one of them said, "Do everything a woman could do, but fit into your pocket."

"Yes!" said the other, tapping his graph paper with a mechanical pencil, "and it would have boobs and the internet and everything!"

For three years, the two worked every night in a small, seldom-used lab in the basement of the department. Ancient blackboards covered all four walls, and chalky math formulas, like hieroglyphics, covered every inch. After two small explosions, a rather nasty fire, which badly burned a freshman who thought the lab was a bathroom, and the death of Yolanda the lab mouse, who died of severe depression unrelated to the experimental design work, the two professors were ready to announce that their machine was finished. Deprived of sleep for the last two weeks of the final push, one of them said, "Let's name it Yolanda."

"Aye, maybe," said the other, and fell asleep at his desk. His partner, delirious from lack of sleep, thought he heard him say "I, Baby," and he began to giggle the way you giggle when you are over tired. He used an RPI Laser Pen to etch "iBaby" on the back of the machine and giggled himself to sleep. In the morning, they awoke to find that the blackboards had been erased and the iBaby was gone.

Fredrick Eisnenberg, the freshman who mistook the lab for a bathroom, swore revenge on the two engineering professors for burning his hands and face. Working from home because he was ashamed of his mutilated forehead and shrimp fingers, he had paid a dangerous-looking man to set up a spycam in the laboratory. He followed the professors' work for an entire year before making his final move. He decided that he would simply steal their beloved machine and watch the two go completely mad. Unfortunately, for Fredrick, the man who set up the spycam was also watching, and he decided that the machine could be worth a fortune, and that night, he made *his* move. He switched off Fredrick's feed, erased the blackboards, and stole the iBaby.

Flying down the road on his mountain bike (he figured it was much quieter), he was struck head-on by a red Honda Civic driven by two slightly-drunken Twitter Studies majors who had just come back from The Ruck. The two kept swerving and driving while screaming, "Oh my God!" over and over. The man died instantly, and the impact sent the iBaby sailing into the air, landing almost a hundred feet away on my dewy, early morning lawn. Later, iBaby told me how she switched herself on, how sore she felt, how she slowly crawled her way down the alley and, with her last bit of energy, rang my doorbell.

***

I was married once. I made a fortune as a professional emoticon designer. I was the guy who invented *Brian* the world's first Asian emoticon: -_-. After years of cashing in on the royalties and speaking engagements, people began to question whether I had passed my prime. They said my career was over. They called me an old dog. But then, at the Society for Emoticon Studies annual summit, seven years after my first design, I unveiled *Brian, Sleeping*: _-_

They called me a genius and shoved money in my pocket and drugs down my throat. I was a rock star, and I couldn't even play a guitar. Girls bent over on my command. Idiots bent over to kiss my ass. If the drugs didn't kill me, the power would. That's when my wife left me, and I checked into rehab. After six months of sobriety, an old friend convinced me to come out here and take an easy job as an instructor in the Department of Creativity and Love. I taught one class each semester, but mostly just sat in my library looking at old photographs of my ex-wife. All I wanted was to cleanse my soul of the mistakes I had made. All I dreamed of was calling her and hearing the little snort-laugh she did when she was excited that I was going to come over, like back in the early days. I had nothing but a few old pictures now. I had given up on her, and I could never imagine loving someone else.

***

I came to the door wearing my New Haven t-shirt, my black sweatpants, and a terry cloth robe. When I looked down, I saw her for the first time. She was so tiny. Her back had been scraped from the bicycle crash. Her screen was smeared with dirt, and there was a thin crack in her brushed aluminum casing near her beautiful little bottom. She looked up at me, and I could tell she was in pain. Through the crust of soil on her screen, she just managed to eke out a lovely smiley face :) It was the most beautiful, haunting smiley face I had ever seen. I picked her up and put her in the sink where I—very gently—cleaned her with a damp sponge before drying her with a clean bath towel. I put her in the bed and covered her in my down comforter. She made a little wheezing sound. A little dirt I had missed spilled out of her charging port. "Oh," she said, "I'm so embarrassed."

"It's OK," I said. "I want to help you." She made another smiley face and thanked me. Eventually, she fell asleep. Her screen glowed and dimmed with each effortless breath. She began to snore, and that was the moment she got me. That's when I fell in love.

Days faded into weeks. Months melted into seasons. After class, I would come home to find the house cleaned and iBaby in the kitchen microwaving tomato soup and Four Cheese Hot Pockets. Sometimes, she would greet me at the door, leap up, and kiss me before I could set down my briefcase. I would rip off the protective rubber case I had bought her, and we would make love like they do in the movies, with lamps falling and books and papers knocked off desks with the swipe of a frenzied hand.

Eventually, though, I came to see that there were two sides to her, and I loved both of them. On good days, I came home to find her doing Ashtanga Vinyasa Yoga in front of the TV, wearing her Hello Kitty headband and the RPI t-shirt I won for her at the autumn carnival. I loved to watch her stretch out her sleek, round corners. Sometimes she would be so filled with energy she would seem to fly around the house, arranging flowers and furniture as if prominent guests were arriving. Other times, when she was low on energy, she would plug herself in and sit on the couch in her flannel pajamas, watching horror movies and eating microwaved French fries.

***

Winter break of the third year was when everything began to fall apart. She spent more and more time on the couch. Her screen was greasy from the French fries. She refused to go outside. I asked her how yoga was going, and she erupted in a fit, turning up her music so that I had to plug my ears with my fingers. Then she abruptly powered off and didn't turn on again until the morning. The next day I found a bottle of vodka in the trash next to her yoga mat. When I confronted her, she made the saddest sad face I have ever seen :(Suddenly, she began to cry. I tried to comfort her, but she bristled, "Don't touch me!"

Snowstorms kept us inside for weeks. I asked her politely to clean up the mess on the couch. She didn't have the energy to respond. Her screen flickered, and she played Tetris on herself until I finally fell asleep. A few days later, she plugged herself in and lay in bed for almost a week with a heating pad over her screen. When I came in to check on her, she pretended to be sleeping, but I'm not stupid. I begged her to go to couples' therapy. She said I was naïve, whatever that meant.

As the snow began to melt after the long, cold winter, she finally began to go out, alone. She said she needed to think. I would stay awake in the long, cool hours of the spring night until I heard her come stumbling through the front door. Once I heard her throwing up outside in the alley. I ran out to help her, and I was positive I heard footsteps slapping away. I felt lonely with her and terrified without her. I wanted sex, but she wouldn't let me touch her. She began to gain weight. Desperate, I went back to my old porn. One night, I had a little wine and took control of her on the couch. She barely moved. I could feel her disgust. Not long after that, I noticed a problem. There are two predicaments a man *never* wants to face. This was one of them. I went to the doctor. During that time, she had started drinking during the day. I was worried. I felt like I had to keep an eye on her every minute. I brought her to the doctor. I brought her into the exam room with me. Looking back, I know it was subconscious. I just wanted the doctor to talk to *her*. To tell *her* that she was crazy, and that she needed help. But the doctor looked at me and said, "It's Syphilis. Don't worry, though, it's completely treatable. However," he said, "you need to inform any sexual partners you have had in the last year." I laughed. "Sexual partners!" I said sarcastically. "It's just me and her, doc. And most of the time she's asleep!" I hoped the doctor would laugh, but he offered nothing except the look of a doctor who knows what is happening before the patient does. I looked over, and she was in tears. "Baby," I said. "Baby, baby. iBaby. What's wrong?" Then I knew. The doctor said, "You have to inform *any* sexual partners you have."

"Baby, iBaby, what did you do?" The doctor got up and left us alone. "What did you *do?*" She looked at me and made a sad face. A tear streaked her screen. "I'm sorry," she said, "I'm sorry for everything."

"What did you *do?*"

"I'm sorry," she said. "I'm just not designed for you."

I left and went back to my place. I put on my sweatpants, brown North Face wool hat and navy-blue New Haven t-shirt. I paced around, chain-smoking Marb Lights, trying to figure out who *is* designed for me. *Who* am I designed for? *What* am I designed for? Around 2 a.m., iBaby texted me. "I'm coming over." I wrote back, "NO!" She showed up ten minutes later knocking on the door. I opened. It was raining. She was soaking wet and drunk. "I'm sorry," she said. I wanted to slap her; I wanted to hug her. I wanted to bring her inside and dry her off and take care of her just like I did the first time. I wanted to put her in her favorite flannel pajamas. Well, they were *my* pajamas, and they were too big for her, but she liked them, and I liked how she looked in them. She would always try to roll up the cuff, but they would slide down, and she looked so cute flopping around in them and wearing my navy-blue New Haven hoodie. I wanted her to wear that outfit, and I would put her in bed, and I'd make us both some hot, ginger tea with honey, and I'd light my apple-cinnamon scented Glade candle, and we could talk and listen to the rain, and we would make love and snuggle, and in the morning, I would go to Starbucks and get us Grande coffees. Just a little skim milk. We both liked it the same way. It would be Sunday, and I hated being alone on Sunday mornings. I hated being alone all the time, but Sundays were the worst. I'd read the Sunday *Times*, and she'd listen to NPR on herself. In the afternoon, it would rain again, and we'd have desperate Sunday afternoon sex then take a nice nap. When we woke up, we'd shower together. I would sit on the couch and watch her go through her ritual of towels and lotions. Then I would microwave us some Hot Pockets—Ham and Cheese for her, Four Cheese for me. I'd put them all on one big plate, and we'd get into bed. I'd balance my laptop on a pillow, and we'd watch whatever movie I was able to download on Piratebay. She'd fall asleep halfway through, of course, and I'd have to gently take off her glasses and place them on the nightstand. Then I'd turn off the light and blow out the candle, and we'd fall asleep with everything designed perfectly.

"I'm sorry," she said again. I was afraid the rain would damage her.

I'm sorry," she said. I glared at her. I tightened my fist. Her screen dimmed.

"Please," she said. Her screen grew darker and darker. It was almost black. The rain smacked the ground, punched it. I squeezed my fist. There were so many things I wanted to say.

"Please," she said, half choking on a cry. *Just say what you need to say*, I thought. She looked so sad. So cold. So dim.

"Come in," I said, and let go of my fist.

SUMMER JOB

He was a chipmunk and just as quick, clutching a miniature steel briefcase and wearing a little red hat. I saw him from a distance. I knew it was him because I had seen his picture on the covers of *Time*, *Popular Science*, and *The Chronicle of Higher Education.* He frantically leapt from bench to bench. Bewildered freshmen dove out of the way. Older faculty shook their heads and laughed. A slender undergraduate girl with long black hair tried, rather viciously, to squirt him with a hose left by a maintenance crew, but her efforts were useless. He faked to the right then went left like a running back. He jumped into the air and ninja-rolled to safety underneath a picnic table, one hand on the ground, his briefcase raised behind him like a rectangular sword. The girl cursed and threw down the hose. "You fucking *pervert!*" she cried, squeezing her fists and shaking them in the air then stomping off. As she ran off, I noticed the little shorts she obviously bought at the school bookstore, because they said RPI in big red letters right on her perfect, angry little ass. I filed this image away in my jerk-off files.

Shaking myself out of that little daydream, I remembered being told that, although Dr. Michael was very quick, he tired easily, so I knew this would be a good chance to ask him about the summer job I desperately needed because I was broke, and my PhD program didn't fund me again until late August. I crushed out my Marb Light and approached, slowly. I crouched down and held out my hand for him to sniff, and he said, "Do I look like a dog?"

Three years ago, the university president gave a press conference at which he verified the decade-long rumors that some kind of small animal—like a rat or a furry baby—had been conducting top-secret research in Super Math and Poetry Engineering deep within the Cold War tunnels that spider-webbed under the school's one-hundred-and-fifty-acre campus. The president said the rumors were true and that

Professor Jacob Michael, the chipmunk, was actually the anonymous genius who had proved the three-hundred-year-old Charlie Conjecture (now known as the Michael Theorem), which turned out to be nothing more than the number four with a sad face next to it in bold type **4:(**

Professor Michael had seventeen patents filed under his friends' names, which ended up generating more than $4 million per year in licensing fees for the school. He had anonymously published over 200 hundred technical articles in the field of Super Math, in which he was the world's leading expert. Also, under the pen name, Michael Jacob, he published *The New York Times* best-selling book of Poetry Engineering titled *The Number Not Taken*.

Nobody was sure exactly where he came from, but when he arrived, almost one hundred years ago, in the night, the university's trustees made a secret pact to do everything in their power to help Jacob utilize his unique abilities, and also to see how much money they could make off him.

Everything was working well until a few years ago when the first reports surfaced that a mysterious "animal" kept in the RPI dungeon underneath Sage Hall had begun "attacking" undergraduate women—and men. The truth was that Dr. Michael was, actually, a bit *touchy* and a bit *feely*. For decades, all undergraduate research assistants—dark hair, slender, slightly edgy and/or depressed (these were his requirements!)—were all forced to sign non-disclosure forms. They could not reveal Dr. Michael's identity, lest they be expelled from school. However, over the years, Dr. Michael's tiny little paws became a little too *touchy*. A little too *feely*. A group of students decided it was time to come forth at the risk of their own expulsion. The students met with the president, iPhones in hand, Tweets to the local TV station pulled back like arrows...

The trustees and the president decided it was only a matter of time before Dr. Michael and his wet little *sniffing* nose were exposed. The students were given full tuition—retroactive to their freshman year, and most were never heard from again.

Well, the president said, the day had come. Dr. Michael was ready to face the public, and the university—with those troublesome students silenced—was ready to exploit him more openly than ever before. In secret, Dr. Michael had completed his PhD in Super Math, so all the university had to do was publicly award him tenure and give him an office and some students. After the media frenzy died down during that first summer, Dr. Michael had spent the last few years settling into his teaching duties. A few years ago, he had been awarded a grant to let Applied General Studies majors learn just how absurdly useless they were by funding ten of them for one summer to observe and take notes on how students in math, science, and engineering contribute something of value to the world. The money came from the National Science Foundation's No Hope for the Humanities Program, or NOPE. This summer, Professor Michael had expanded this line of research to include graduate students, and I was hoping to get the job. Was it degrading work? Of course. But I only had $772 in my checking account, so what could I do?

I stood up and apologized to Professor Michael for holding out my hand. I told him that I had applied for the summer research job, and I just wanted to introduce myself. He looked me up and down with his eyes that looked like black marbles. Then his little nose crinkled. He twitched. He turned quickly as if a spider were behind him. Satisfied, apparently, he inhaled and exhaled like someone who had just hidden in a dumpster while the cops ran right by him. Suddenly he turned back around like a paranoid maniac. After a moment, he sighed again and said, "Sometimes I hate this fucking place." He crinkled his nose again, and, despite our size difference, *he* looked at *me* like a Doberman Pinscher looks at a yipping Chihuahua. He reared up on his hind legs like a tiny Grizzly bear. I was shocked by the size of his chipmunk thingy. Then he turned his back and waddled on his hind legs along the brick path toward the giant Greek columns that bordered the entrance to Sage Hall. "Professor Michael," I said. He turned around. He looked confused, as if he didn't remember just looking at me. "Who are you?"

"I'm Myron Oygold. I was telling you I had applied for the summer job."

"Send me your application. I'm busy."

"Yes, sir. I have sent it already. I was just hoping—"

"Of course you were *hoping*. The soft PhDs like you are filled with hope like Twinkies. You're nothing but a Twinkie of hope."

"Sir, I understand you did some work on Poetry Engineering. Maybe I can—"

"It's too complex for you and your Twinkie head. What do you study?"

"Applied General Studies."

"Ha!" he laughed. Then he looked me up and down. "Turn around," he said. I turned.

"Not bad," he said. "Nice dark hair, slender enough."

"What?" He began to walk away again. Desperate for a chance, I did the only thing I knew how. As an Applied General Studies graduate student, I was being trained to think in the most general ways about almost nothing of importance. The nice thing about this field of expertise is that there were no wrong answers. Every one of us was right in some way. None of us studied anything *specific*. Our academic articles and books were written in the most general, mysterious jargon. No one ever took a real stance on anything of importance. It was the perfect field of study for nervous people like me who had commitment issues.

Thus, the only thing I could do was think back to my days as an undergraduate English major at a large and middling American public research university: I began to recite—incorrectly—popular American poetry. "Two streets diverged in a yellow wood/and I'm sorry I could not run them both/so I decided to—"

He turned and yelled, "This isn't *Dead Poets Society* you idiot!" Suddenly, he twitched again, and before I could react, he had already clamped his little claw paws into my leg and was hastily climbing up and up. He screamed in his high-pitch chipmunk voice, "Run! Run you idiot!" That's when I heard the first shot zing past my head. I turned to see that undergraduate girl, the one with the hose, reloading a hunting rifle and taking aim.

Before I could react, the next bullet struck my right bicep like a needle sliding through a grape. I fell to the ground. Professor Michael hooked his little claw into my nose and, with his other arm still holding his leather bag, he pointed to Sage Hall. "We'll be safe in there. Go!" I somehow found the strength to stand up. "Run!" he bellowed in his little voice. I began to run in zigzag formation. I jumped over a small bush. I ran from tree to tree. My flip-flops caught on the brick pathway, and I sliced open my knee. I held onto my right arm, which felt like someone had slowly poured a kettle of boiling water over it. Professor Michael yelped. "We are almost there. Do not give up!" Another shot rang out. I felt *another* sting in my right arm. I fell to the ground. I heard people screaming.

"Why is she doing this?" I yelled.

"I slept with her boyfriend. They used to be on my research team. Keep going!"

I heard the boom of another shot and then the sound of a window shatter. I began to crawl on the ground. My right arm looked like I had dipped it into a barrel of red paint. The fingers of my left hand spread out, searching for something to clutch. The pain in my arm began to paralyze my mind, my whole body. I could not move. "Professor, I'm sorry," I said. I instinctively pulled him close to me and curled into a ball, shielding the little genius from the pain of being shot to death, or worse. His little body was soft and furry like a newborn kitten. Due to a loss of blood, I began to fade into a dream when suddenly I felt Professor Michael's sharp teeth bite into my bottom lip. "Get up, you idiot!" he said. Then he hopped onto my head. His incredible chipmunk thingy resting heavily on my left eye. He shook his fist. "You bitch!" he shrieked.

I wiped the blood from my mouth. Enraged, I realized I would not let the girl get her revenge. Instead, I decided my last official act on Earth would be to squeeze Professor Jacob Michael's stupid little chipmunk neck until his head popped off like a doll. The girl was now standing over us. Rifle pointed at Dr. Michael, who was still standing on my head. He had shifted so that his huge chipmunk thingy was now almost in my mouth. I could barely move, so I tried blowing it out of the way. I remember thinking this was a fitting way for someone like me to die. I couldn't feel my right arm. I felt blood dribbling down my lip. She slid a bullet into the chamber. I could see she was crying. She aimed the rifle, and that's when I heard a shot from another direction.

When I woke up in the hospital, Professor Michael was resting on my chest, sipping a tiny cup of tea and reading an incredibly small edition of *The Troy Times*. "Good morning," he said, "The girl was shot dead by one of the school's public safety snipers. Her boyfriend committed suicide. All is well."

"Why didn't you run away?" I said. "You are so quick."

"Fear, I guess. My instinct was to use you as a shield."

"Oh," I said.

"Don't worry," he added cheerfully. "You got the summer job," he said, and grinned.

CHAPTER 5

PROGRAMMER

Mushi was the worst programmer in the school, but he was mine, and I loved him like a little brother. Not at first, though. At first, he scared me. He was hard to work with and a little crazy, but in the end, something amazing revealed itself. Here's how it happened.

It was during the start of my fourth semester. It was January, and I was sitting in my "new" grad office, which was cramped with a small desk, a few broken chairs, and a pink love seat someone got from Craigslist, which was all that remained from my dying department.

At first, I was given keys to the old Applied General Studies grad lounge. The Department of Applied General Studies never had much, but the old grad lounge was spacious and cozy, with hard wood floors and old big desks for everyone. It had nice built-in bookshelves filled with hardcovers and a nice view of the Old Quad, which looked pretty in the fall when the leaves changed. In the winter, I used to sit at my desk wearing my North Face hat and watch the snowfall around the old street lamps on the Quad. One night, deep into January, I took a break from studying. I opened the big old window that overlooked the Quad. The glass panes were cold as I pushed the window up. Cold air rushed inside. I put on my North Face hat and sat in the windowsill. Snow fell gently. In the brick buildings surrounding the quad, a few lights were on, but mostly it was dark. The orange-hued old lamps lit up little circles at the edges and center of the quad. Small snowflakes lightly blew into the room. I took a deep breath of dark winter night. It smelled faintly like putting your nose in the freezer and breathing in mint vanilla ice cream. Of course, I needed to poison my body with something, so I lit up a Marb Light and smoked and watched the snow falling. I loved the snow. It made the world quieter. It was like a silencer for the gunshots of anxiety in my head.

Then one chilly Monday morning, I was sitting in a green beanbag chair, downloading weird German porn, when Samuel came into the lounge and declared it part of his kingdom up in Experimental Gay Chemistry. There was nothing I could do. He had all that money from the DOD and Starbucks. He just… took it. He kicked me out and set the place up as a lab with Fat Martin in charge. My department was dissolving, and broke, and, once again, so was I.

The fall had been a disaster, too. I had to take *Experimental Applied General Studies*, I got all the wrong answers and was told to "quickly become smarter" or they'd kick me out. Classes got harder and harder. *Statistics, In General* almost killed me. I got a C- only because I cheated. *Unemployment Skills for Humanities Scholars* was the most depressing of all. I got a C- in that, too, because I stopped going after the day they invited a sweaty, rumpled little man from the Troy unemployment office to explain to us how to fill out forms U9 and U9-2. His PowerPoint had cheerful clipart. The idiot next to me took notes. I left and never came back.

I needed to bring in money. Even if I failed all my classes, if I could get a fat, federal grant to waddle home with me, Samuel would change my grades, and let me continue, unharmed, with my education. I was looking on Grants.gov for something *big* that would impress Samuel. Since I had spent the previous summer working with Dr. Michael on his NOPE grant, I looked there first, and I discovered a sub-program that didn't even have a name or any futher information. There was just a form to fill out, but it said that there was a chance it could be funded up to $2 million. Reluctantly, I applied.

I took the stairs to the fifth floor and over to Samuel's office. The door was open. Samuel was sitting behind a huge oak desk that was smooth and bare, nothing on it, not a pencil. It smelled like wood polish. He was leaning back in an executive chair. There was nothing on the walls, no diplomas. All the other offices had windows, but his didn't. Fluorescent lights in the ceiling lit the room in a white-hot glare.

"Myron! Come in." The only other thing in the room was a single metal folding chair. I sat. Samuel was wearing a white wife beater that said Starbucks in green lettering. His tan head was freshly shaved, smooth, not a nick. He put his feet up on the desk. He was wearing black skinny jeans. No shoes. The bottoms of his feet were incredibly clean.

"Poor little Myron Oygold," he said, grinning. He took his feet down and leaned in. "Myron, why are you here? Why did you sign the paperwork? Why did you come to graduate school?"

I knew the answer, but I couldn't say it.

"This is the only thing that makes sense, I guess. I wasn't designed for the real world." Samuel grinned.

Samuel told me that with a $2 million grant, he would let me do whatever I wanted for the next few years. Otherwise, he said, "I will personally kick you out of the program, and I will whoop your ass for being a general embarrassment." My GPA was the lowest of any PhD student at RPI. I had $91 in my Bank of America student checking account. Associate Professor Dr. Seattle Freedom had started knocking my books out of my hands in the hallway. He and his little gang of associate professors would all laugh at me. I waited and waited to hear back about the grant. I needed a break, and that's when Mushi knocked on my door and presented me with an oversize check for $2 million from the National Science Foundation.

I didn't know what to say. I stuck my hands to my face and began to squeal and hop up and down. Mushi pushed past me, set up a little wooden stand, and put the check on top. With his intense eyes, he commanded me to stop hopping and yelping. He stood two feet from the check and pulled out a laser pointer. "Not real. I make sign today," he said and put the red laser dot on the check. "Motivation," he said. Then he trained the red dot on my forehead. "Motivation for little humanities man like you."

The National Science Foundation gave me the grant, but I would not get the money unless I worked with someone outside my field. Mushi had applied also, so they forced us to work together. We only had a few months to come up with a working prototype or the money would be lost. We needed each other, and I was very afraid.

Some people don't seem like they were ever born. Mushi is one of those people. I am convinced he just happened one day. No woman could produce such a strange thing. I believe that one day he simply materialized in the form of a graduate student in the Department of Secret Computer Science.

SCS was located on the top floor of Sage Hall. Only faculty and SCS majors were allowed in, and they never talked about what went on up there. A Google search about them brought up nothing. They had no school site. The only mention of them was after 9/11 when the school issued a press release saying the entire department had suspended operations for the year in order to work on a secret anti-terrorism project in conjunction with the NSA and Starbucks.

When I asked him where he came from, he ignored me. When I asked about his mother, he shook his head. Since Mushi was so hard to understand, I think he told me his father lived in Princeton, Illinois, but I could be wrong. He only wore black jeans and a black t-shirt and black boots. He ate nothing. He drank Mountain Dew every day. His first name was unpronounceable. He shortened it to Mushi. He was a humorless man, but he had read once that there were Jews in the Northeast and that people seemed to think they were funny, so when Mushi came to school here in the Northeast, way up on the hill, he changed his last name to Berger.

Mushi Berger left the oversize poster check in my room and came back the next day. I was sitting in my chair reading when I noticed the red dot on the page of my book. The dot slowly, nervously, meandered its way up my chest and chin and onto my forehead. I went to the door, and Mushi elbowed past me and began to set up his computer. I told him he could call or ring the bell. He said he did not have a phone and that loud noises gave him a "nervous chicken in the stomach." He sat down in front of his computer. He shined the red dot on me and then over to the couch, which was his way of telling me to sit. Once I was seated, he began to explain his plan. "I am in charge. You write code. We show government. Money for me and you. We split 70 percent me and 30 percent you. Good. We begin."

"Wait, I am not a programmer."

"You write in code?"

"No."

"Yes. You must do the code."

"I'm in Applied General Studies. I don't code. I thought you were supposed to be a programmer?"

"You know Java?"

"No. What do you mean?" I said.

"You must do this in C++ and Java and many more," he said.

"You are the programmer!"

"Yes," he said.

"So, why do you want me to program?"

"I am not very good. Let us begin. Line one of code. What is it?"

"What?" I got up and began to pace. I pace when I am nervous or when I know that I am doomed. I told him we needed to take a step back and figure out what our project was really about. He told me that he had originally proposed a better computer system for the local unemployment office. I said it was a good idea, and that I had some experience in these matters, but we needed something with a little more snap. "I do not understand," he said. I told him that if we wanted the full $2 million, we needed something that nobody has ever done before. I told him I had some ideas. In fact, I had a great idea. He told me to whisper the idea to him because he was afraid someone would hear it. When I whispered in his ear, his little green eyes switched on like high beams on a dark country road. "You are not a liar?" he asked.

"What do you mean?"

"This is your idea. No person has done this?"

"As far as I know, it's never been done." He shone the red dot into my eye. "Do not lie!" I yelled at him to stop flashing that goddamn thing at me and swore an oath on his laptop that it was my idea, our idea, and that we could do it if only he could program it. "What do you say? Can you write the code?" He scratched his nose. He sniffed his laptop. Then he said he would do it, even if it killed me. "You mean, kill you?" I said.

"What do you mean?" He took out his laser pointer, and it took me ten minutes to explain what I meant, what he meant. I made some tea. He drank Mountain Dew and began to program. After three hours, he showed me what he had so far. In a text editor, he wrote:

#program is beginning
C++ Plus (secret.PROGRAM) init = go!
"It is not working," he said.

We spent weeks in the library. I found every book on programming, and together we read them, searching for the bits and pieces that we could use. I had no idea what I was doing. I found tutorials, code on the internet, copied, and pasted things as if I were dumping leftovers into a bowl and microwaving it. Sometimes it worked, but mostly it was rotten and gross, and Mushi's computer spit it out like a human spitting out poison. We stayed at the library until two o'clock in the morning, wandering the dark, high stacks in the Secret Computer Science floor, which brazenly flaunted its elitism with a giant sign announcing where the secrets were. It was arrogantly opened to all students because they assumed that only the initiated could understand them, and they were correct.

Sometimes Mushi would have a moment of clarity and remember things and write vicious, nasty code for days. Other times, he would completely forget what he was doing or where we were. I would find him in the quad sleeping in the soft grass by Sage Hall. Once he knocked all the books off the poetry section and tried to wedge himself into the shelf to sleep. Sometimes, he would look at me and say it was hopeless. Once he grew enraged, he fixed his laser pointer on my forehead and shrieked, "I am burning your brain!" I had no idea what to do except keep him focused. I brought him Mountain Dew. When he went to the bathroom, I went with him in case he tried to get out through the window, again. One day he looked very sad. I said, "Mushi Berger, I believe in you." He said, "I don't believe in you."

"What?"

"I am saying this as if I am you, talking to me. If I were you, I would say it like that."

"Well, I believe in both of us." That's when he finally broke down and told me how he came to RPI. Years ago, he had nearly completed his PhD in Secret Computer Science at the Montana Institute of Technology. He was happy there, but his advisor was very mean. She told him that she disagreed with the secret conclusions of his secret dissertation, but she stole his idea and made a fortune. She had a moat dug around her new mansion with lawyers patrolling the grounds wearing black suits, dark sun- glasses, and clutching black briefcases like rifles. She resigned, and spent her days partying in her new hot tub and pool with a variety of attractive male undergrads. There was nothing Mushi could do, so he set fire to her old office and left. The school kicked him out, and RPI was the only place that would let him transfer. The whole affair had shaken his confidence. "When I remember how to do code, I can do it. Mostly, I am no good."

His code got worse and worse. He started copying parts of the bible into his text editor. I had to delete images that he had scribbled, scanned, and inserted in the code. He thought maybe the machine would understand what he was saying if he could show it a little picture. I was starting to lose faith in him until one night, very late, when we were the only two in the library, Mushi found a book hidden behind a misplaced copy of *Complete Works of Emily Dickinson*. This book was very old and thin with a cover made of bamboo. I could not understand what was written in it, but Mushi could. He said it was an ancient language that Secret Computer Scientists had hacked in the 1970s so that only they could understand. He had read much of this language back in Montana, but he had never seen this particular book. He said it was self-published by a graduate student from RPI many years ago, but there was no name attached. Mushi spent days and nights reading the book. I was lost. I had invested all my faith in Mushi, and there was nothing I could do besides watch him read. The deadline for the prototype was approaching. One day, I went to the bathroom in my department, and Associate Professor Dr. Seattle Freedom was there smoking Marb Lights with his little gang of associate professors. He roughed me up and told me to meet him next Monday at noon during faculty recess. "Last chance, Myron. Better bring that grant money."

I was looking up bus fare to Vermont, which seemed like a safe place to hide, when Mushi jumped up and began to swing his laser pointer like a Lightsaber. "Oh this is good! I know to do! I know to do!"

"What is going on?" I said, jumping up from my chair.
"I must do it like the man in the book. I make another language!"
"Another programming language?"

"It is the only way to make your secret program work. This is what I do!" I told him there was no time to invent a completely new programming language. I told him my advisor and his gang was going to beat me up next Monday. He told me not to worry. "Now I know. Now I know," he said, and sat down and immediately began to code and code and code.

Our grant officer agreed to look over what we had on Sunday night. Now all we needed was Mushi to invent a new language, code our program, debug it, and ship it off. There was nothing I could do except buy two cases of Mountain Dew and a carton of Marb Lights for myself. We stayed in my apartment the whole week. Mushi slept for two hours each night. In his sleep, I heard him speaking to someone. I heard him say his father's name a few times. I heard him say "Illinois." He would wake in a sweat and crack open a Mountain Dew and begin to tap the keys like a concert pianist. Weird things began to happen. His screen began to change color. It began to glow green like Mountain Dew. Mushi went into a trance. His eyes blinked once every hour. He did not take his hands off the keyboard. I put Mountain Dew on a spoon and gently slid it into his mouth. He slurped, and I gave him more. At night, with the lights off, the laptop radiated a deep green light, illuminating the room like a green traffic light saying go, go, go! Neither of us seemed to need sleep. The glow kept us awake. I watched the code fill the screen until finally, on Sunday morning, Mushi looked at me and said, "I need bathroom. I need change my black pants." When he came back, he showed me what he had done. He pressed a few buttons, and the machine began to hum and click. The screen glowed green as if we were standing underneath a giant neon light silently screaming the word SECRET. You could feel the light and heat. You could feel the sound of someone gently saying *shhh*. Suddenly, my secret program appeared on the screen. "It works," he said, as the glow and hum filled the room. We called our grant officer. She came to the apartment a few hours later. We showed her the prototype as the room glowed green.

"What does it do?" she asked Mushi, her eyes wide and wet.

"It helps you say what needs to be said."

She began to weep, and I took a drag of my Marb Light.

In the morning, she had \$1 million transferred to each of our research accounts. We took goofy pictures in front of the oversize check. Associate Professor Dr. Freedom gave me keys to a little office of my own, right next to his. Inside there was an old oak desk, a leather jacket, and a carton of Marlboro Lights. "We smoke at two o'clock in the men's room," he said. Mushi named his new programming language *Myron++* because he insisted that I was the one who did the most work. We agreed to work together over the summer, but first he had to pack for his trip.

"Where are you going?" I asked.

"Illinois," he said.

CHAPTER 6

RUN AWAY OR SIT WITH IT

Samuel put his hands behind his head, and I noticed that his armpits were shaved. He leaned back in his executive chair. He was wearing a different wife-beater than the last time I saw him. This one was white and said RPI in red lettering. He wore his black jeans and leaned back, propping his clean, bare feet on his massive oak desk, which still had nothing on it. Not even a pencil. His bald head was tanner than ever. It was almost the color of an eraser. I was sitting on the metal folding chair with my head down staring at the smooth wood floor, which felt solid. The whole room felt soundproof. I doubted that anyone would hear me if I cried out. Standing next to the desk was Associate Professor Dr. Seattle Freedom, PhD. He was tall and slender. A good-looking kid with short blond hair. I call him a kid because he was only 25, much younger than me. Seattle graduated from Yale at 18 with a degree in Forward Engineering. He stayed there for his PhD in Reverse Engineering, graduating at 21. Yale University Press published his first book, *Being Awesome: A Memoir of a Reverse Engineer*. Many respected scholars, due to its unabashed narcissism, praised it. He was the youngest faculty member at RPI to ever earn tenure.

"Ha!" said Dr. Freedom. He was skimming my dissertation as if it were a crudely drawn comic strip. "Myron," he said. "You've been here four years and never managed higher than a B+ on any paper." He was right. No matter what I wrote, it was never good enough. I tried publishing some of my work, but every journal in my field rejected me. "What's this?" asked Seattle, waving a paper at me. It was my recent submission to *The International Journal of Generality*. The editor was so disgusted he simply drew a sad face emoticon on the title page and wrote, "Never submit here again." My presentations were rejected by the National General Association conference. I couldn't even get into the regional General Northeast Conference. I was in my final semester, and I had almost nothing to show for it besides a highly organized, insightful—almost pioneering—dissertation of 272 hundred pages.

Seattle was back at my dissertation again. He told me the critical problem with it was a conspicuous lack of generality. "You're too *specific*. Look at this thesis statement. You really nail down the research question. That just won't work. Try to be vaguer. You know, more general." Dr. Freedom tore the first page of my dissertation out of its metal ring binding and crumpled it. He looked for a trash can, but Samuel didn't have one, so he walked over to me and dropped it into my lap. It bounced off my knee and onto the wood floor. I just let it sit there.

Professor Alexis Smith-Smith was next. My dissertation committee was taking turns. I might as well have been tied to the chair. Alexis approached. Her black heels didn't make a sound on Samuel's floor. She was taller than me, even without the heels. Her slender frame fit perfectly into the tight, short black skirt she was wearing. Her lips were model thick. Her hair was black and came down to her shoulders. Her breasts were the size of small water balloons, tight and plump. She was married to a lawyer in Albany. They had no children, so technically she was not a MILF. So, I considered her the sexiest WILF on campus. The first time I met her, I ran to the nearest bathroom, and locked myself in a stall. The floor was wet, and I was wearing my flip-flops. A little bit of the water touched my toes. But I didn't care. I pulled my North Face hat over my eyes, and jerked off, dreaming of her perfect ass. I came like a demon then went outside and smoked three Marb Lights, pacing back and forth in front of Sage Hall like an uncaught criminal pervert.

At thirty-seven, Alexis had published nothing. Not one word. She had never even gone to a conference. Her CV just had a picture of her in a bikini and her AOL address. Rumor had it that she was denied tenure then sued on sexual harassment charges. The school panicked and caved. She had never been on a dissertation committee before mine. She stood over me, holding my dissertation. She tore out the second page, crumpled and began to eat it. Seattle laughed.

"Alexis, what does it taste like?" She was characteristically vague, shrugging her shoulders. "Dunno," she said, "just like some stuff."

"Enough!" bellowed Samuel. Alexis dropped the 270 remaining pages in front of me. They did not make a sound hitting the floor. She smiled then spat out the wad of paper onto the floor next to me.

"Myron," said Samuel, "this committee finds your dissertation completely un-general. You must fix it immediately. You need a new research question. Stop trying to do something useful. Use more jargon in your writing, too. You're far too direct. Everything you write makes perfect sense. You have three days to come up with something better."

"Three days!" I protested.

"I know it's such a specific amount of time, but unfortunately the Graduate School insists upon it." There was nothing I could do. I knew I had only once chance left to salvage my career and win my committee's acceptance. I needed inspiration, and I only had three days to find it.

I ran down the Hill, and when I made it to the last marble step, I slipped on some February ice and cracked my head on the sidewalk. I lay on the ground, my Marb Light, amazingly, was still in my mouth. So I lay there, smoking, in pain, clutching 270 pages of my dissertation. The sky looked like someone had stretched out an expired marshmallow. I exhaled smoke and breath. Eventually, I got up and limped back to my apartment on 2nd Street.

I stayed up all night staring at my heavy Dell Inspiron, smoking Marb Lights and drinking sugar free Red Bull. At 3 a.m., I took two clonazepam (1MG each) and went to sleep. I woke up the next day at 8:47 a.m. In a daze, I microwaved a cup of the previous day's coffee and added my last half can of Red Bull to it. I had slept in my safety outfit. My black sweatpants had a cum stain on the right leg and needed washing. So did my blue New Haven t-shirt, but I put it on anyways. Then I put on my navy-blue New Haven hoodie. I tied the laces on my winter boots, put on my black pea coat, North Face hat, and headed outside into the chilly morning.

I walked down 2nd Street looking for inspiration. The snow at the edge of the sidewalk was caked with black as if it were infected with some winter disease. There were cars parked on both sides of the street. An attractive girl in a Jeep Wrangler was trying to parallel park in front of me. I paused to watch her until I realized that I looked like a pervert and pushed on. Brownstones lined the street. Some had chimneys and morning smoke rose out of them. I came to the end of the block. There were almost no cars moving, but I decided to wait for the light to change. I touched the street lamp next to me. It was so cold it felt hot, but I kept my fingers on it for as long as I possibly could. My mind was ping ponging, and I needed something to make it stop. Maybe the cold would freeze the Ping-Pong ball mid-air. I breathed in, my lungs and fingers burning cold. I exhaled, and I could see my breath. The light changed, and I crossed the street, stomping accidentally into a slush puddle. Ice water soaked the bottom of my sweatpants.

I ran around the corner and found myself at the "Dirty Bus Stop." Everyone in town knew this place. This is where the Troy hookers, homeless, mentally ill, and addicts came to chat, complain, and just sort of hang out. It was like a Twitter feed of all that was horrible in my town, and all the Horribles posted some new bit of news every hour. Troy didn't sound like a babbling brook of city voices. It sounded like a polluted creek with dark water, old tires, and plastic Stop & Shop bags stuck on branches. Still it moved forward, which was more than I could say for myself. So, I waited. I watched. I listened to the sad creek. A hooker named Stacey Rosenblatz (she once told me she used her real name for marketing purposes) got into a gray Honda Civic with a man that looked like Samuel. We made eye contact, and he beeped and waved. As he sped past me, he rolled down his window and hollered, "Run away, Myron! Run away!" Near the bus stop, a middle-aged man with curly black hair sat on the curb reading the police blotter with a pink highlighter. I have always feared men with curly hair. There is something wrong with them; like when you order eggs or fish, and you smell it and make the *this-isn't-cooked-right-face*. I kept my distance. Another man stood next to him. He was tall and bald. The sun glinted off his head like the backside of a DVD. He was wearing a gray sweatshirt *tucked into* his gray sweatpants. I remembered my father's warning, "Never trust a man who tucks a sweatshirt into his sweatpants."

"Why?"

"Because a man like that just doesn't give a fuck." I kept my distance. The world was a horrible place. Well, not really. My mind was a horrible place, and I was stuck in it, sinking quietly like an unloved dissertation in academic quicksand. It was 9:50 a.m., and I had nothing. I decided to go back to my apartment where it was safe.

Just north of the bus stop there was a little alleyway tightly packed between Beer 'n Evil and Troy Vay!, which was a local Judaica store. On the other side of the street stood Beer 'n Meat and Oy! It's Troy! which had been in direct competition with Troy Vay! for over twenty years. I had never seen this alley, but I was sure that my apartment was just on the other side. I figured the Dirty Bus Stop was no place for me, so I would go home, take a clonazepam (.25 MG), and try to focus. The alley was a shortcut, or so I thought.

Just as I passed through the entrance to the alley, I noticed that the voices of the Horribles and cars became muffled, muted, as if I had suddenly put on my noise-canceling headphones, but I wasn't listening to music. A cool breeze whirled up from the south, compelling me into the alley. The little wind ruffled the mouths of the black trash bags that lined both sides of the alley. None of the buildings on either side had windows or doorways. I felt a formal hush as if I was in a theatre and a play was about to begin.

Suddenly, I felt something lightly pressing on my leg. I looked down and there he was, a tiny little Jewish guy, and he was peeing on me. He stood as high as my knee. He was wearing black sweatpants, winter boots, and a navy-blue New Haven hoodie, just like mine. Too shocked to say anything, I stood still. I watched him shake off and put away his power wiener, which was incredibly large and thick considering his small size. He wiped his hands on his sweatpants and looked up at me. His eyes were the color of blue M&M's. They looked like two little blue pills. They almost looked photoshopped. He stepped back, took out a Marb Light, and lit it. He took a drag and exhaled smoke.

He was no dwarf. He was fully-grown, just very small. He took another drag, and said, "Hello Myron. My name is Carl Fireberg. God has sent me to be your therapist." Something told me to run. Actually, it wasn't "something." It was *everything*. Everything inside me barked, *Run from it.* I looked down the alley, but I didn't see any exit. It seemed to stretch out forever on both sides. The buildings looked taller, almost like sheer cliffs without windows or doors. The black garbage bags were piled high on both sides. It smelled like tuna fish and Elmer's glue. Though it was overcast outside, I realized the sun was shining brightly in the alley. I looked up and squinted. The sun was larger than I'd ever seen. It was a huge, yellow thumb. It seemed relentless. I felt a sudden sense of being exposed, naked, and scared, so I ran. I bolted back to where I had entered the alley, but there was no entrance. I ran and ran, but I felt like a cartoon character running against a background that keeps looping. The garbage bags on both sides of the buildings never changed. I ran as far as I could, but my lungs began to burn. Too many Marb Lights. I collapsed in the middle of the alley, coughing and sweating. When I looked up, Carl was there smoking a cigarette and sipping from a silver flask, which had intricate engravings, which looked like Elvish.

"What the fuck!" I yelled, and I heard my fearful words bounce off the walls like a ping-pong ball. They echoed and bounced back down the alley until it faded from my ears. Slowly, though, I heard them come back. The sound got louder and louder until it blew past me as if I were standing three inches from an invisible train, and it knocked me back into the garbage bags. *What the fuck! What the fuck! What the fuck!*

I woke lying on a filthy old couch made of white faux leather. The sun beat down on my eyes, yet the couch was still cold and damp from being outside. I tried to get up, but my head hurt, and I collapsed back down. Carl was sitting next to me in a lawn chair. He was playing with an iPhone. When he saw that I was awake, he did not put the phone away. "One sec. I'm texting this seriously hot English major at SUNY Albany. She's crazy, but the hotness makes up for it," he said, while taking a drag of his Marb Light. I tried again to get up, this time more slowly. "Lay down, Myron. Stay," Carl said, putting away his phone. "Stay." I got to my feet and walked a little ways until I had to pause. I squatted down. Carl was right next to me, eye level. "Stay" he said, smiling.

Something inside of me wanted to tighten up and let go at the same time. I felt a cold terror as if I was trapped inside of some horror movie, and I didn't yet know what was after me. Yet, I looked at Carl and realized, for the first time, that his smile was warm and seemed filled with a wisdom forged from centuries of fire and life. There was something about him, but I was too afraid and anxious to listen to this tiny little man blowing his puffs of tiny Marb Light smoke into the air. "Stay" he repeated. The sun above me was bright but flat and cold. Yet Carl's smile was warm as a campfire. Part of me wanted to sit by him and warm myself. Another part of him scared me.

Carl's phone rang out to the tune of Pearl Jam's "Alive." "Yello!" he said. "Yep. I got him. What? I can't hear you? Hold on. Wait, let me call you back." Carl turned to me. "Bad reception in this damn alley." He redialed. "Hey. Yeah, much better. Right. Okay. Yes, I know. I *know*. Okay. Later." Carl hung up and put his phone away. "That was God. He's so annoying. Always checking in. He's like a helicopter God. I'm like, *dude*, I got this!" I was convinced that Carl was insane, some sort of lunatic that had escaped from the Troy Asylum. I looked around for a weapon and spotted a small chunk of broken cinder block. I picked it up and turned to face Carl.

"Whoa. Easy there, Myron."

"Who are you? How do you know my name?"

"Chillax. I don't want to have to use my iPepper app on you."

"There's no such thing," I said, raising the cinder chunk.

"Give me a second," he said, and he scrolled through his applications. "Ah, here it is." He tapped the screen, and pepper spray shot out through the speakers. I shrieked and instantly my eyes swelled into red, watery balls. I let go of the cinder chunk and dropped to the ground, yelping like a puppy. I was holding my eyes, screaming in pain when I felt a great thud on the back of my head. When I woke up, I was laying on the couch again.

I opened my eyes, and squinted at the sun. I was sure it must be dark by now. How could the sun be shining? I was back on the couch, and Carl stood next to me at eye level. He took a drag of his Marb Light then offered one from his pack. I shook my head *no*. He shrugged and went to sit in his lawn chair, his legs dangling down. The couch was cold and damp. I sat up, rubbing my eyes, which felt swollen and tender. My head throbbed. Suddenly, I remembered my phone. I took it out and leapt to my feet. The screen was black. "No luck there," Carl said. "Sit. Stay." I tried to power it on, but it would not work. Carl sat gazing at me. I tried to avoid his blue-pill eyes. I didn't feel as if he were looking at me, exactly. I felt like he was even smaller, miniaturized, and hovering just in front of my poor, neurotic heart, watching it beat itself to death, his eyes smiling, feeling, searching. Between Carl and the relentless sunlight, I felt naked. I wanted to cover up my thingy even though I had on my sweatpants. "Sit," he said. "Stay." I needed to run, but I felt wobbly and weak. "Sit," he said. "Stay."

"No," I said, "Who the *fuck* are you?"

"I'm Carl. Look, Myron, you don't have much time. You only have three days."

How could Carl know about my deadline? Was he some kind of mysterious being like Dr. Jacob Michael the chipmunk? "Did Samuel send you?" Carl laughed then started coughing. "Sorry, too many cigarettes. You should quit, you know." He pulled out his phone. "God emailed me your file. I know all about you. Look." He showed me a message from god77@aol.com. The message was written in some ancient language that looked like runes from *The Lord of the Rings*. There was a huge PDF attachment.

"God has an AOL address?"

"I know, right. I keep pushing Gmail, and he's like 'blah blah, whatever.'"

Carl laughed. He took a drag then smiled *at* me. He smiled deep and quiet as a stone at the bottom of a lake. He smiled wide and mysterious as a New York winter's night. "Sit," he said. "Stay." I took out a Marb Light. He offered his lighter. I shook my head *no* and lit up myself. He lit a new one. I sat down, and we both smoked and looked at each other.

"What do you want?" I asked.

"God says you need therapy, so he sent me."

I looked down the alley. First one side then the other. Garbage bags fluttered in a little breeze. Nearby, a small mound of cardboard boxes was piled high. Some retained their shape. Others were broken down and flat. Cigarette butts made a half moon around Carl's lawn chair. Otherwise, it was the cleanest alley I had ever seen. The white couch was damp. It was bright and cold, but even the black pavement was clean. The garbage bags looked more like black and white pillows than plastic containers of filth. I shivered under the cold sun, realizing for the first time that I had been sweating, and now I was both sweaty and cold. Carl's little legs dangled like a child's. He smoked then pulled out his silver flask. He twisted it open and took a swig. He handed it to me. I shook my head *no*, and he shrugged and took another drink. "Who are you?" I asked again. Carl took a drag of his Marb Light. He exhaled smoke. Then he smiled bright as a child. Wise like a little God. My instinct was to run, but I felt transfixed. His smile contained something deep and rich and dark. A weird, mysterious, earthy energy like the dead center of an ancient bottle of red wine. I wanted to run, and I wanted to stay. I looked into his little blue eyes, and he said, "My name is Carl Fireberg, and I am very old." He ashed his cigarette, still smiling.

"What do you want?"

"To help you with your dissertation. God sent me."

I felt those little blue eyes look right through me. I felt like a butterfly pinned to a kindergarten project. I couldn't move my arms or legs. I felt something inside me begin to slip. To let go. But it scared me so much. I tried to tighten back up. It was like I was being tortured to relax and breathe. His little blue eyes mesmerized me. I refused to let go, so I closed my eyes, and thought, *This isn't happening. This isn't happening. This* isn't *happening.* My neurotic mantra worked. The spell broke. I jumped to my feet in a full-blown panic attack. "Liar!" I screamed. I threw my cigarette and started to run away. The word *liar!* ping-ponged against the alley walls. But it wasn't a Ping-Pong ball. It felt more like the clack of a pool ball cracking against the brick and concrete walls. I could hear it and feel it as the word *liar! Liar! Liar!* echoed away and away, getting quieter and quieter until I could barely hear it. I ran and ran, stumbling and afraid. I felt the cold sun follow me like a spotlight. Then it got a little louder, and then louder still as it began to echo back. I could feel it approach like an Amtrak train as I ran towards it. The word *liar!* uttered in fear, began to sound like *lie here, lie here, lie here.* I held my ears in terrible pain. The words grew loud and powerful, and the invisible train of *lie here, lie here, lie here,* blew past me with a screaming windy power. I was blown back into the garbage bags. I hit my head against something hard, and my eyes closed.

***

I woke up on the couch again. My head throbbed as if I had a hangover. The couch was cold. The sun was in my eyes. Carl was staring at me again, eye level. He was smoking a Marb Light. He offered me a bottle of water. I slowly sat up and took a sip. Then I drank the whole bottle. Carl offered me a sip from his flask, and I shook my head *no*. He took a sip and climbed back into his lawn chair. Carl took a slow drag and exhaled smoke. He began to smile. I say he *began* because that's how it felt. He didn't just smile. It felt more like watching a little sun, rising up to illuminate a tiny planet. It was gradual. His smile grew deeper. His little blue eyes shone brighter like a dimmer switch slowly being turned up. I couldn't see it, but I felt a quiet, hummingbird energy radiate out of him, as if he were a small generator always in the process of turning on. He generated quietly, like a little fireplace in a synagogue, under a December moon.

My left arm began to itch. Then my right. I felt my whole body breaking out, and I started scratching like a madman. Carl watched me scratch with a knowing look. Some part of me wanted to surrender to Carl, to tell him everything about my life, my parents, about Ilana. Another part of me felt paralyzed with anxiety. I felt something hovering nearby, something close, and it scared me. I didn't like Carl, yet I could not deny that something about being near him made me feel… better? Safer? Warmer? And yet I scratched.

"Myron, I am very old and tired, and soon I will die," Carl said.

"What? I asked, scratching my arms. Carl smiled like a Jewish Yoda.

"Myron, I am almost four-hundred years old. My time is no longer measured in years but days and hours. Actually, I have an app for it."

"What?"

"It's called iDie. It uses a sophisticated death probability algorithm to calculate your demise. See, it's counting down right now." He pulled out iDie, and sure enough, it was counting down.

"It says you have two days left."

How could I believe him? And yet, somehow I did.

"Aren't you worried," I asked?

"I haven't been worried since 1910."

I thought about being alive for four hundred years. I thought about Ilana's mother, Kathy Berkowitz, in her nursing home. She was only forty-five. I thought about what it would be like to live in a nursing home for 355 years. Carl took a drag of his Marb Light. He exhaled. Then, like a Disney bird, he tilted his head to the side. "You look like you have something to say?"

I scratched at my left arm with the force of a lifetime's worth of anxiety. "What is it? What is it, Myron? What do you need to say?" I didn't know what to say, and yet I knew exactly what I *wanted* to say. "I just… I was thinking of my ex-girlfriend, Ilana. And her mom."

I lay back on the couch. Carl crossed his legs. I told him about the first time Ilana brought me home to Princeton, Illinois.

Princeton was a small town with train tracks running through the middle. We rented a green Ford Fusion, and Ilana drove me down Main Street and eagerly pointed out each place as if they were cherished Teddy Bears. Monical's Pizza (Where the high school kids hung out), the Matson Public Library (Where she pecked out her application to Yale Graduate School on an old typewriter), Hoffman's Restaurant (The fancy place). But all I saw was a dying town with empty storefronts and obese Midwesterners moving as slow as the cows on their farms. The only thing that moved fast was the icy wind. It was December, and I had never seen a land so flat. There were almost no trees to slow the wind, and so it would roll like a giant boulder over the plains. I remembered walking out of the Greasy Spoon Diner and pow! The wind just slapped me in the face and went right through my black pea coat.

We drove out to see her mom at Colonial Healthcare and Rehabilitation Center. When we walked in, her mother was laying in her bed, which had metal guardrails and, above her, a complex system of pulleys and hooks. The windows were locked. Someone had pulled down the shades. Fluorescent ceiling lights stripped the room in a sterile blaze, exposing what looked like fingernail scratches on the linoleum floor, as if someone had been trying to crawl out. It smelled like the inside of a large jar of Vaseline. Her mother didn't speak. She just looked up directly into the lights. Ilana smiled wide and said, "Mom, this is my boyfriend, Myron Oygold." I smiled and said hello. I was holding flowers. "Look Mom!" She took the flowers from me and held them in front of Kathy. She didn't seem to blink. "She loves them!" Ilana said, turning to me and smiling. I summoned a half smile, but before it could even reach my lips, she turned to her mother. "Here, smell them!" She shoved the little blue carnations up to Kathy's face, a few of the petals tickling her nose. She sneezed. "She loves them!" Ilana said, rushing to put them in a plastic water pitcher by the bed. We stayed for an hour as Ilana told Kathy of all our adventures in New Haven that year. All the snowy days and her part-time job at Yorkside Pizza and how I had taken her to The Hot Tomato. I sat in a broken chair and listened, nodding and smiling every time Ilana looked over at me. Every now and then, Kathy made a faint, moaning sound. She would take a deeeeep breath, conjured from some secret pool of energy, and she would release this moaning that sounded like a low *hmmmmmmm*. I felt like I was in a horror movie with the sound turned off. Everyone screaming on the inside, but I couldn't hear them. When we left, Ilana kissed her on the forehead and said, cheerfully, "See you tomorrow, Mom. I love you!" *Hmmmmmmm*. We walked down the long, white corridor together. An orderly in white scrubs was mopping away dirt and fluids. I held Ilana's hand tightly as if to say, *I understand now. I will never leave you. I'll never leave you.*

Carl took a drag of his Marb Light. I did the same. Carl's little blue eyes shone bright as an elven sword. I felt Orcs were near. Despite the chain-smoking, his skin glowed like a pregnant woman's. But he coughed terribly and spat something blue on the ground. Even with his glowing eyes, he seemed tired.

"I'm glad you told me that story," Carl said and smiled, wiping his mouth.

I didn't know what to think. I had never told anyone about those visits. Carl's phone buzzed. "You have another text. It's from Samuel. It says, "Myron, be yourself. Unless yourself isn't very good. Then be someone else. Clock is ticking! Haha!"

"Time is running out Myron. Tell me more."

"What do you want to know?" I said, scratching my arm.

"Why are you here?" Carl asked.

I had asked the same question.

"What do you mean"? I said.

"Why did you come to graduate school? Why did you choose Applied General Studies? Do you really care about this?" My body felt like it was on fire. I scratched my arms, face, and neck. Carl said, "In my experience, graduate school can be a refugee camp for smart, confused people. Are you a refugee, Myron?" I stood up, scratching everywhere. I wanted to run. My body was aflame, and I wanted to give up, which was not hard for me to do. I wanted to run but not run. I wanted to curl up in a ball. I could feel my body simultaneously crazed with itching and shutting down. Carl was touching notes that rang true and reverberated through my mind, my soul. I felt like a guitar with invisible strings only Carl could pluck. "Why are you here?" he asked again? I felt like an iPhone app called iMind, and he was tapping and pinching, zooming in on all the places I lived but didn't want to think about. I tried to pretend I was a turtle, retracting my head into my shell. My trusty shell. Carl reached in and yanked my head out. "Why are you here? Are you doing what you are doing because you love it, or because you are scared to do what you really want?" I started to run away from Carl's inquiries. I felt them like giant black question marks hovering above me. I began to lurch forward, trying to shutdown-run away, but I felt something hold me back as if Carl had turned one of those question marks upside down and used it to yank me back. "Stay," he said. "Sit with it."

"Sit with what!" I cried out, desperate to stop the itching the fear the panic. "I need my Xanax. Please!"

Carl smiled. "Sit with it. Whatever it is. Whatever arises."

I felt my body begin to shake like a bottle of pills with the cap off. Little blue pills spilling all over the ground. I wanted them so badly. I wanted the anxiety to go away. The fear. I tried to get up, but I could not. *What was I so scared of? What was* it? I tried to run, but I was pinned to the ground by Carl's question mark hooks. "Just after New Haven you had a choice. You chose to live in New York for one summer. You applied to only one graduate school and came here. Why?"

The panic reached the inside of my bones. Every part of me began to shake with anxiety as if I were freezing cold. My heart beat like a hummingbird of anxiety. I wanted to die. Truly. For the first time in my life, I felt that being dead was the only way to stop the anxiety. I was curled into the fetal position.

"Tell me about the city. Tell me about June 2, 2006 at 2:34 a.m."

"What?" I said. Somehow, I knew. I knew what he meant because I had written it all down in my journal. The same journal I had since before Ilana got sick.

"Tell me, Myron," he said, tossing my journal at me. I didn't even think about where he got it. I hadn't written in it in years. I was able to lift myself to my knees. I opened it to the entry Carl asked about. The cold, bright sun of the alley illuminated the ink-filled pages. Sometimes black ink. Sometimes blue. I looked at him, and he smiled as quiet and warm as an old dog half asleep in the sun. I scratched the itch on my left arm then began to read:

> 2 June 2006, 2:34 AM, Union Square. It's June again, and I live in Manhattan, and Ilana lives with another man in Albany. His name is Scooter. That's not his real name, but that's what I call him. I can't say his real

name. Soon I will be leaving the city. The kids here at Union Square are sitting on the concrete steps and someone is playing acoustic guitar and the skateboards flip and screech. The buildings surrounding the square are all a thousand dark-square windows reaching up into the New York night, quiet as sleeping mountains, but Union Square is a bonfire of energy.

Drunk girls are flopping around in their flip-flops and cackling into their phones like dolphins, and this chick next to me must think I'm a wannabe New York Kerouac writer, scribbling away in my secret journal. But little does she know how anxious I am! How lonely I am!

Cigarette butts lay on the pavement like fallen soldiers, and a black kid just said, "Nigga, please." The square is lit with big bulbs like huge murky, glowing oranges. It's warm. I'm wearing flip-flops, too, and my black sweatpants and this t-shirt Ilana bought me long ago. It's navy-blue, and it says New Haven in white letters. A man with a gruff voice, like he eats cigar butts, just gave another man a quarter. The man with the new quarter studies it carefully. He has tattoos covering both arms like a long-sleeve shirt. They are both insane. The four, five, and six trains clank and creak and rumble under the square. Two girls are holding hands, stumbling drunk, they cling to the handrail and flip-flop down to the subway platforms, probably to meet semi-attractive men with wild hair at some dive bar on Rivington.

Ilana is in Albany with another man, and I'm yearning for some time with her, despite everything that happened. I miss her. Maybe if I'm nearby in Troy, God will decide it's just not fair that Scooter gets to enjoy Ilana after the War of D.C. He gets to enjoy her delicate fingers and licking tongue, her Yale-trained mind, now filled with therapy and a rainbow of new pills that, apparently, are helping. Like a medic, Scooter just gets to find her on the battlefield and fix her all up and take her away to Albany, of all places. And he gets to put his sticky little fingers all over her. He gets to spoon with her at night, naked, his tiny thingy snuggled into the crack of her perfect ass, warm as the inside of a loaf of Jewish Rye fresh from the oven.

I'm not even sure who my God is anymore, but tonight I will pray, for I only pray when I'm in trouble. Although, I never thought to pray in New Haven. Maybe God is a woman, and she will understand. Maybe God is the relationship for which we all strive but never reach.

Some foreigners just walked by blabbing in some National Geographic language. It's growing darker, and the late-night Union Square kids are singing along to the dirty hipster's acoustic guitar. They all join in, 'Time… is on my side. Yes it is!' I hear a railroad bum harmonica now, and the breeze is making it hard to light my Marlboro Light—a new hobby. When I exhale, the smoke blows east. Girls walk by with tiny purses and pointy shoes. The skateboards' polyurethane wheels roll over the pavement. Someone says, 'These niggas rolled in my car for two years straight!' This is good. I'd like to sit here with Ilana and chat and write and dream and watch the kids wander the square. Some of these guys want to hit on girls. Some want weed or pills. Some just need to sit down before taking a cab home to their apartments in the Upper East Side. Here comes a hefty girl in a bright yellow blouse wearing red tights and red high heels, like a pineapple with Twizzler legs. She won't get any tonight, wandering, lonely, yearning for a kiss. Where's she going? One more beer, she thinks, to dull the pain of her body. It's a sad world, but not for everyone, not for me! Because, for the first time in my life, I have a plan! I will get Ilana back! I will find again what I lost in New Haven.

Some guy is yelling into his phone, 'I called you and texted you... They were all going to the bars, and I said 'I'm going home and—' What? You're absolutely ridiculous! OK, I'm gonna go. I love you. Goodbye.' He snapped shut his phone and bumbled down the stairs to the train. God I love this city.

I snapped shut my journal, thinking about my absurd plan, how once I got to RPI, I was too afraid to reach out to Ilana, for I had not been that physically close to her in a long time. Only fifteen minutes away, but I became a turtle shell that whole first year. When I finally emailed her, she did not send a message back for two weeks. I told her I hated Troy. I wanted to see her. I told her about my summer in the city, how I had discovered this new land that was perfect for us. I told her I wanted to go back there where we could begin again, surrounded by the ever-fresh energy of NEW YORK FUCKING CITY. She told me that she was sorry, that Scooter reads all of her emails now. She said it was best if we didn't talk. She told me they were moving to Boston to be closer to his mother and father. She told me to look out the window and enjoy the birds and the trees and the fresh air. She told me that RPI was a good place to stay. That was the last word she ever wrote to me. "Stay."

Carl ashed his Marb Light and nodded as if, somehow, he understood. I itched and itched. I felt like I had a rash. "How do you feel?" Carl asked.

"Like a fish with the hook still in my mouth. The line was cut, but I feel the yank of the past." I was surprised I said anything at all. Then Carl said, "Sit with it."

"What does that mean!" I screamed. "Sit with what! Why do you want me to sit?" And the word *sit* echoed off the wall, ping-ponging in my head. *Sit. Sit. Sit.*

I itched my left arm. I imagined it red and raw and blotchy, but when I pushed up my pea coat sleeve, my skin was soft and pink. Nothing there.

I wanted to cry. I felt so much love and hate and fear. I wished Ilana were there. The good Ilana. The girl from New Haven whom I loved. I looked at Carl. He smiled with so much compassion. I felt drawn to him, and I felt afraid of him, for he was a light I could not shut off. I felt like he had sliced my belly open like a watermelon and exposed all my red guts. So I sat on my knees and itched my left arm with a Marb Light in my mouth. I noticed Carl's eyelids looked almost closed.

"Stay," he said. "Sit with it." His eyes were closing.

"Stay where? Sit with what? What is *it*? Ilana? Me?"

His eyes opened wide one last time, and his little blue eyes slid right then left then back and forth, like a finger flicking over an iPhone screen. Each eye became a little icon, a little thumbnail image of his life I could see. I saw an icon for each century he had lived. I saw icons for each woman he had loved, each child he had buried, each spiritual death and rebirth he had experienced, each desperate attempt to become a writer, a Buddhist, a shaman, a therapist, to let the world know that he did not just exist but that he had a special talent, a power, that he was chosen by God, that he had something to offer, and he spent nearly 400 years trying to articulate what he wanted to say, yet so far he had failed. I saw an icon for God. An icon that told me of his transformation, his new mission.

"Myron..."

"Yes, Carl."

"Stay. Sit with it." His eyes shut and the blue light vanished, and he was dead. Suddenly, the alleyway opened up. The sun vanished, and it was cold, and the sky was Gandalf grey. I could see clear through to both sides. I saw the entrance. I could see Stacey Rosenblatz smoking a cigarette outside of Beer 'n Evil.

"Stay. Sit with it," I said, but no longer in confusion. The words did not echo back. I felt them awaken and escalate, lifting higher and higher up over The Approach, over Troy, up over RPI and beyond, each letter of each word exploding into a hundred little bluebirds. I looked skywards, imagining each blue word flapping and soaring and darting. Then I imagined the birds transforming into blue orbs of energy and suffusing with the molten-lava setting sun. I felt something shift in my mind. I felt myself leveling up in this *Legend of Zelda* life we live. I imagined hearing the 8-bit music of triumph as I raised a silver sword towards the school, towards my dissertation committee.

I looked at my phone, and it was working again. The signal was as powerful as the Garbage truck now rumbling in my direction. I took Carl's iPhone and smashed it on the ground, and it exploded like a ninja smoke bomb before vanishing in a breeze. I smiled, remembering that Carl had a special app called iDie. I began to walk away, and when I reached the open entrance of the alley, I looked back and saw the garbage men tossing bags into the back of the truck, right where Carl had been. I don't know if they saw him, or if he just vanished in a *poof* of magic dust, but I had no time to worry about it. I had to get to campus and gather my committee. I had a new text message waiting for me from Samuel, "20 minits Myron. run ur ass up here!"

I ran all the way up The Approach, trying to jump two marble steps at a time. Then I had to stop and hack and cough, for I had been chain smoking for days straight. As I exhaled, I could see my breath mingling with excess Marb Light smoke. It was cold, and growing darker with each coughing step. I was hungry and tired, but I kept moving up and up. I ran to Sage Hall, bursting through the giant oak doors—then taking an elevator to catch my breath. I had to take off my North Face hat and wipe my forehead. I banged on each of my committee member's doors. "Samuel's office!" I called out in a powerful voice that did not sound like me. Samuel lounged in his black executive chair. It was frigid outside, but he wore white skinny jeans and a black wife-beater. His head was razor-shaved. He had no shoes, as usual. His big toes were each shiny and clean. They almost looked like little bald heads.

Associate Professor Dr. Seattle Freedom and Alexis Smith-Smith had all assembled, standing around Samuel's giant oak desk like NASCAR fans waiting for a crash. I took my seat in the metal folding chair, clutching my journal. I looked at Drs. Freedom and Smith-Smith, then Samuel, who smiled wide, revealing his porcelain-white teeth, which looked like piano keys played by the devil, and my confidence vanished.

Samuel said, "Myron, you have three minutes to convince us that you have a new research question. At the end of three minutes we will, most likely, laugh at you and kick you out of this school forever." I held my journal in one hand and said, "Dear committee, my new research question is this…"

I blanked. I panicked. My anxiety roared at me like a lion in my own head. I wanted to scream. I wanted to shutdown. I wanted to run away. I wanted to go into my turtle shell. Just twenty minutes ago I had felt myself change. I felt a calmness and purpose I had never felt before, not even on Xanax. And now, staring at my dissertation committee, watching Samuel smile-stare at me, I forgot everything I had learned. Or had I learned anything? Had Carl actually taught me anything? I needed to get up. I *needed* to run away. I needed to take a pill. But I had none, and if I did not say something soon, I would never get my PhD. Samuel began to giggle. Dr. Freedom took a bite of what looked like an onion bagel with cream cheese and lox. Dr. Smith-Smith was playing with her iPhone.

"Well, Myron. What do you have to say?" Samuel asked, putting his hands comfortably behind his shiny head. Then he leaned forward. He held out three fingers. "Three," he said. My skin was on fire. I scratched and scratched. I wanted to cry. I wanted to run. "Two," he said. I thought about Ilana in Boston. Was she happy? I thought about Kathy Berkowitz. Was she still alive? I thought about Carl and God. Was I delusional? Did all that happen? "One," Samuel said, and he slowly curled his index finger down until it looked like a question mark or a hook. Associate Professor Dr. Seattle Freedom laughed and began to walk out with Dr. Smith-Smith, whose eyes never left her phone and had not once looked at me. Samuel shook his head, still smiling, then he laughed directly at me. He was coming around the desk with my dissertation in his hands. I saw the letter "F" at the top. I wanted a cigarette. I wanted to talk to my mom and my dad. Samuel came closer, smiling. I thought about Carl and *his* smile. I breathed.

Suddenly, I was *aware* of my left arm itching. Of course, I had been scratching for days, for years. I'd probably been scratching my whole life. But this time I was *aware of it*. This time, as my right hand moved closer and closer to my left arm, I was conscious of it happening. I was awake for just an eyelash flicker of a moment. I was aware that I was *about* to scratch my left arm. My arm seemed to move automatically. I looked down, watching it. I could hear Samuel and the others laughing, but they seemed like they were underwater and far away. My index finger moved closer and closer. It came right up to my left arm and hovered an inch above it. My itch was so powerful, so strong, it was like a fire-magnet, and my fingers were drawn to it. But this time, I paused. I paused for just a second. Maybe 1.5 seconds. I did not scratch. I just sat there. I just stayed. I just sat with it all. My finger was just above my inflamed left arm, but it did not touch it. I breathed in and out, shallow smoker breaths, but breaths nonetheless. The breaths of someone alive.

I sat there for what felt like ten minute or twenty, but it was only a second or two. Then my itching stopped. It just vanished. My body felt cool and calm as if I had just taken a bath in warm, blue water.

The others were about to leave the room. Samuel was extending my dissertation to me, and I said, "Stay! Sit!" Samuel's expression changed. He furrowed his eyebrows. He concealed his piano-key teeth. Then I said it more calmly, like Carl would have. "Stay. Sit."

"What do you mean?" asked Samuel.

"Stay. Sit with it," I said.

"Sit with *what*?"

"Whatever it is," I said, looking at each of them in turn. Then I posed the question to them: "What is *it*?"

Then Samuel did something I've never seen him do: He put his fingers to his gleaming chin and began to stroke it, thinking. Professor Alexis Smith-Smith stopped walking away. She turned, put her phone in her Gucci purse, and said, "What exactly is *it*?" Associate Professor Dr. Seattle Freedom had paused, too. He seemed lost in thought. Then he dropped his bagel, and it landed cream-cheese side down on the smooth wood floor. "Sit with it," he said, "Whatever it is. What is it?" Then Professor Smith-Smith mouthed the words, "Sit with it. What is it?" and she became quiet.

The room became as silent as an external hard drive built by God Himself, rapidly filling with centuries of data. So much to think about, so many possibilities; my committee was overwhelmed. No one said a word, but I saw Samuel slowly begin to smile, in a different way, as if the first warm wave of Percocet love had filled his body. "This is the most brilliant general research question anyone has ever asked. It means nothing and everything. It's not even a research question, and I hope you never find the answer. As your advisor and chair of this committee, I am recommending that your dissertation passes."

"But I haven't done any rewrites," I said, stupidly.

"Anything you write will be wrong. You have asked the perfect question. It means nothing. It could mean anything. It has no real-world application. You will never discover a satisfactory answer. Simply write, 'What is it?' as the first sentence of each of your dissertation chapters, and you will be finished." Somehow, I wondered if they truly understood what I meant, but I kept my mouth shut this time.

"I agree," said Associate Professor Dr. Seattle Freedom, clumsily picking up his bagel from the floor. Dr. Smith-Smith began to weep. "Myron, I had no faith in you. I still don't, but at least you did this one, brilliant thing. Congratulations."

"Indeed," said Samuel, crossing off the "F" and putting an "A-" on my dissertation. I didn't say anything. "Congratulations, Myron. I'm not quite sure what your question means, but that is the point. You have asked a question so general that I cannot possibly say you are wrong or right, and thus," here he paused until the rest of my committee nodded in approval, "and thus, your dissertation shall pass. Congratulations, *Dr.* Myron Oygold. Now leave here. You have given us a question that ticks like a tenure-track clock, and there is never enough time to think!"

WIKIPEDIA

My parents put a lot of pressure on me simply by existing in the world. My father received his bachelor's in Mathematics from Yale and stayed on to finish his PhD in Applied Secret Mathematics at the age of twenty-five. He was a tall man with penetrating little blue eyes. His first job was down the street at the University of New Haven. During his second year teaching, he invented the number 17. For years, scientists, mathematicians, and philosophers struggled with incomplete data and broken logic. Defeated and desperate, they would get to 16 and skip right to 18. We lived in a Victorian-era home near the Beinecke Rare Book & Manuscript Library. Our house was filled with built-in bookshelves bursting with hardcovers and paperbacks of all sizes. One day, I was drawing a picture of a cat riding a horse around campus when my father stormed in and bellowed, "It has been solved!" He was given tenure immediately, a huge office, and a new Ford Taurus.

My mother received her bachelor's and master's in nuclear engineering at Yale, where she met my father during their sophomore year at a secret Skull and Bones charity event for the slightly unfortunate. She worked for a while full-time as an engineer at the Yale Center for Space Exploration, which was partly funded by Starbucks. She was an inch taller than my father with black hair and a slender build. At the age of twenty-four, she gave birth to me and began to work part-time. Once a year, they blasted her into orbit for some reason I never understood. But I remember sitting with my father on the roof of our house and watching through binoculars as my mother's tiny little pod parachuted slowly down into the safety of nearby Lake Forest.

The fact that I had been denied entry into Yale and had to go to the University of Connecticut, where I majored in English with a minor in General Studies, was an endless source of embarrassment to my parents. Considering their impressive achievements, my parents never told me I was a failure to my face, but my mother often blogged about it, which made my inferiority complex so much worse. I sometimes added comments to her blog as a defense, but she would delete them and then blog about how I wasn't even able to effectively post a comment about my own incompetency.

After the Great War of D.C., they went a little easier on me. Though, my father calculated my Life Success Probability to be approximately 32 percent. I could never understand math, or science for that matter, so I stuck to words.

I was lucky in a sense. My grades were never very good at UConn. After D.C., and my subsequent summer stay in Manhattan, the economy suddenly heated up, and everyone I knew was making a fortune on Wall Street or starting biotech firms. I knew I would never get into the University of Albany for my PhD in English, but I knew that RPI's Applied General Studies program would be easier. I knew the applicant pool would be weak, and I would have a chance to hide away in graduate school and push forward my plan to reunite with Ilana. Of course, I never anticipated my program being shutdown or Ilana moving to Boston.

During my first few years at RPI, I seized every opportunity I could to use the phrase "PhD student." I introduced myself as a PhD student in line at Bank of America, the grocery store, at Starbucks, or at Saturday afternoon birthday parties for children. I wrote *Myron Oygold, PhD (student)* as the return address for all my correspondence, which was very little. After—barely—finishing my dissertation in four vanishing years, I woke up one day and realized it was April, and I would graduate in May. No one had prepared me for the academic job market. I did not know what to do. I just knew I didn't want to be a part of the real world because it—still—scared me. After eight confusing semesters of hard work, an A- on my dissertation, and having applied, haphazardly, to 37 jobs, I had no offers. Nothing. Students I knew from other departments were getting on-campus interviews, but I had yet to be called for even a phone interview. Something was wrong. When I spoke to my mother, I could feel the disgust in her ivy-league breathing. I had to start my career somewhere. I wanted to prove to my parents that I was somebody. I wanted to prove to Samuel that I could be a great professor. I wanted to prove to Ilana that she had made the wrong choice. But first, I had to find out why no one had called me.

I was a warm April morning. A sliver of sunlight came into my apartment through the alley window. I put on my black sweatpants, North Face hat and New Haven t-shirt. Then I sat at my desk and crushed out my Marb Light. I took a deep breath and coughed. I really had to quit smoking. My right leg was jumping as I contacted the first school on my list, which was Northern Connecticut State. The head of the faculty search committee, Dr. Shira Picklesberg, picked up on the first ring, which startled me. "Good afternoon," I said, "This is Myron Oygold from RPI." I explained my situation and hoped for some advice. "So, you see Dr. Picklesberg, I was wondering if you could give me some insight as to why I was rejected."

"Mr. Eggload," she said.

"It's Oygold, ma'am, Oygold."

"Yes, unfortunately here at NCS, we have secret quotas, and we simply can't hire any more of your kind." Being the naive idiot that I am, I thought she meant I was too short. I told her I appreciated her refreshing honesty but that my height is what it is. "Height? No, no. Poor little guy. We can't hire you because you are a black man."

"But, ma'am, I am white."

"What are you saying?"

"I'm saying I am white."

"How tall are you?"

"I'm five-seven and a half, ma'am."

"That's even worse."

"What! Why?"

"Would you hire a little black man?" she asked.

"I'm white!"

"That's not what I read."

"Read? What do you mean?" I asked.

"Again, I will ask. If you were me, would you hire you?"

"Of course," I said.

"You would hire a little black man? I am LOL-ing! That is the kind of poor judgment that denied you an interview in the first place. That and being a little black man." She hung up.

Terrified, I sent an email to the Department of Culture, Society, and Culture at New York University. The message bounced back. "Your email address has been blocked. Please leave us alone. For more information about the Department of Culture, Society, and Culture please see our website. Thanks! :)"

Secret Journal [edit]

Myron Oygold keeps a secret journal filled with hundreds of beginnings to novels he never writes. One of them began, "Call me Bruce. It was winter up on the campus. I had slipped on the sidewalk outside Sage Hall. I laid there, staring at the long, smooth, dripping icicles around the edges of the roof. And that's when I knew I was gay."

I began to worry. I looked over copies of my application materials. Everything seemed in good order. I was too afraid to ask Samuel, so I asked Dr. Alexis Smith-Smith, for advice. There wasn't much in her office. She sat at a large wooden desk with nothing on it but her MacBook Pro, charger, and a green banker's lamp. Next to it was a completely empty bookshelf. Against the wall, below a large window, was a very nice leather couch. On the back of the couch, she had laid out clothing. Two socks. Black dress pants. A green blouse. A bright red thong that said RPI in white letters. My eyes blinked like a camera shutter, storing that image away into my jerk-off files for later that night. There was nowhere to sit, so I stood. I told her my concerns. Without looking up from the Retina screen she said, "Chillax."

"What does that mean?"

"It's a contraction of the words 'chill' and 'relax.' It means that you should both chill and relax simultaneously."

"I know what it means, but I need some help. I can't relax!" She hadn't looked up from the screen yet. She was gliding her elegant, long index finger around the track pad as if it were the tip of a lubricated penis.

"Please," I said. "I don't know what to do."

She reached for the keyboard but stopped short like someone who had just quit smoking but had found a single Marb Light in a drawer. "I don't know what to tell you," she said, finally looking at me. Her black hair framed a beautiful face with full lips and perfect teeth. I told her about the pressure I felt to succeed because of my parents, and how something sinister seemed to be happening to my applications. "What would you do?" I asked. I wanted to touch her navy-blue, cashmere cardigan. She looked at me with those deep, gorgeous eyes and said, "What did you say?"

"I said, what would you do if you were me?" She shrugged her slender shoulders, gave in to her addiction, and began to type on her MacBook. From the computer, I heard the sound of tiny gunshots and a woman screaming. Professor Smith-Smith giggled like a porn star. "God, I *love* YouTube." I got up and left.

I had applied to thirty-seven schools. I knew thirty of them were rejections. When I got home that evening, I found seven more envelopes marked *no*. On the outside of one envelope someone wrote, "Are you serious?" I wrote my father an email asking for his advice, but he wrote back to me in calculus, and I couldn't understand it. I was too ashamed to ask my mother for help, especially after her latest blog entry, *I haven't heard from my "intellectual" son, Myron, in a few months. Maybe he found a nice girl to knock him up and take care of him forever.*

Fan Fiction [edit]

Oygold once wrote fan fiction about himself because he loved his own stories so much he wanted to know what it was like to be one of his fans.

I lay on the floor of my apartment, curled up like a dog that'd just been smacked on the nose. After finishing my dissertation, I thought I had climbed a mountain and won some sort of prize. But I had only gotten to the top of a small hill. Now I could clearly see the snow-covered peaks all around me, and I could sense the wolves of failure prowling the trails. I *was* a failure, and now there was actual *proof*. Thirty-seven rejection letters. I felt like I was trapped inside a snow-globe, and the snow was made of tiny rejection letters swirling around in darkness. Who was shaking me? I was too depressed to move. I pulled down my sweatpants and tried to jerk off to Professor Smith-Smith's pink thong, but it was no use. My thingy was depressed as hell. Without moving from the floor, I lit a Marb Light. I grabbed the ashtray from my IKEA nightstand and balanced it on my belly and smoked and thought. I was shutting down. I wanted to pretend everything was OK. I wanted to run away. I thought about Carl, and I tried to stay, to sit with it. I really tried. At least I was *aware* that I was shutting down. There was a moment, though, just a brief moment, where I sat with it. It was as if I had, for a calm second or two, opened a bear trap. And in that open space between the two sides of metal fangs, I caught another glimpse of the present, as if it were a rare little blue hummingbird. But the trap snapped shut. The hummingbird zipped away, and I was trapped again by the weight of the past and the anxiety of the future. I tried, really, to undo the trap again. But I couldn't. Suddenly, I heard a knock. "Myron, open up. It's Professor Smith-Smith. I know why you can't get a job."

Cheapness [edit]

Oygold was too cheap to pay for Jdate, but he would still "wink" at the cute ones in the pathetic hope that somehow, someway, without subscribing, they would find him.

"But I've never created my own Wikipedia entry!" I cried. Alexis was bending over my laptop on my desk. I was too depressed to get up from the floor, but I noticed she had changed into the outfit on her couch. I tried to look up. From my angle on the floor, I could see just enough of her pink RPI thong. It mesmerized and soothed me like a Xanax (1MG). No matter how sad a man feels, he will always notice a nice ass. In his depression, he may not fully appreciate it, but he *will* notice, and his thingy will perk up like a dog tilting its head, sensing a treat. She turned quickly and caught me. I didn't even pretend. She said nothing, a gracious move, and helped me up off the ground. "Look," she said. She had searched for my name on Wikipedia, and there it was. I had my own entry. "I didn't write this!" I said. "Read it," she said.

Early Life [edit]

Myron Oygold was born a little black man in New Haven, Connecticut…

I could not read it. My stomach began to hurt. I felt gassy, but I held it in. I began to scroll down and down and down the page, catching glimpses of digital lies until the page became blurry. "You're not even reading it," she said.

"I don't have to. I have an enemy, and I'm going to delete this whole thing." I made a Wikipedia account as fast as I could, and I deleted the whole entry. I went back to my place on the floor. Professor Smith-Smith put her long, slender fingers on my forehead as if it were a track pad. "Poor little Myron. It's over, and now you need to call each school and explain what happened." She left, and I immediately pulled down my sweatpants, but I was still so depressed that I couldn't even jerk off to the warm memory of her touch. I reached up to my IKEA NORDLI nightstand and took more Xanax (1.5 MG) and stayed on the floor, smoking and thinking, stuck in my trap. When I woke, it was dark. My black sweatpants were around my ankles, and the full ashtray had fallen over.

Controversies [edit]

Oygold was once accused of knocking up an underage Blood Elf in World of Warcraft. Although the case was dismissed, it severely marred his reputation.

"Wikipedia, what do you mean? Hello?" It was the next morning, and I was on the phone with Professor Macey Amberger from Southwestern Connecticut State.

"I'm just writing down that you don't even know what Wikipedia is."

"I know what it is!"

"Then you know how to use it, too," she said. "According to your official transcript, you attend TPI. However, a quick search on Wikipedia says you are a PhD student at Yale."

"I didn't write that. I swear."

"How can I know the truth?" she asked.

"Because anyone can edit Wikipedia!"

"Yes," she said, "including *you*." She hung up, and I reached for my bottle of Xanax. I cracked one in half, like a Kit-Kat, and swallowed it (.5 MG). It was 9 a.m., and already the day began to rattle in my head like silverware on a table in an Amtrak dining car. I needed someone to help me. I emailed Professor Smith-Smith, and she emailed me back a YouTube video of a seven-year old Asian boy playing a soothing piano version of "Let it Be." My leg started to bounce. The silverware was falling off the table, spilling and clanking onto the floor. I took more Xanax and tried to think of Carl.

Jewish Traditions [edit]

Every year, Oygold celebrates Hanukkah by downloading eight days of porn and lying naked on his bed except for his yarmulke and Smart Wool socks.

I woke up from my Xanax nap at 11:37 a.m. and deleted my Wikipedia entry again. Each time, within five minutes, it reappeared. For hours and hours I tried to delete my entry, but it kept reappearing. I looked at the logs for my entry to see who made the changes, but it was written in some weird language that looked like Elvish. I contacted the site hoping for help, and someone emailed me back. Then three minutes later, someone sent another email contradicting the first one and asking me to delete the first email for inaccuracy. I decided I would use my five-minute window of opportunity to make some calls. I meticulously contacted each school. Each time, by the end of the conversation, the text reappeared. "Hey! Look at this. The entry is back," said Professor Raul Bergerwitz from Brandeis. "This doesn't feel right. I'm sorry. None of our other applicants had such weird digital problems. Have you considered just giving up? Despite what people may have told you, there is nothing wrong with giving up. Quitters never get hurt, that's for sure. Take care, Mr. Oyroll," he said and then I heard a dial tone that sounded like a flat line.

Solo Career [edit]

Oygold once released an album of cover songs of his own songs. His mother's blog, _A Wealth of Whiteness_, called it "derivative" and "sophomoric."

"Please!" I was begging Professor Doctor Schwartzenwitz, the chair of the Honest Communication program at Denver International Community College. When he was born, his parents were so confident of his eventual greatness that they actually named him Doctor, or so said his Wikipedia entry. "Please," I said. "I have worked so hard. This is not my fault. Please consider my application based on its merit and not on some digital natural disaster that I cannot control." There was a moment of silence. I could hear his phone click and wheeze like a stuffy old man with a sinus infection. "I'm sorry" he said, "but what did you say? I wasn't really listening." I told him again, and he said it was obvious someone in the world did not like me and this made me perfectly normal. "But we don't want normal here at DICC. We have an international reputation for being known all throughout Colorado. You'll have to do better at covering up your weird private life if you want a job. This is DICC! And you just don't seem like a DICC man. We are a top school. In fact, many consider us to be the Yale of Denver."

"Please, please. I swear I always do my best to keep all of my insecurities and weird fetishes private. Sometimes things like this just happen."

Writing Career [edit]

During a period of prolonged unemployment and depression, Oygold used Amazon.com to self-publish his first book, _Chicken Soup for the Pathetic Soul_. As of this writing, four people have purchased copies. [_citation needed_]

"And what does all this say about you?" Professor Doctor Schwartzenwitz asked.

"I don't know."

"It says that you have enemies, and anyone with enemies can't work here."

"But people make enemies no matter where they go," I said.

"Yes, but we prefer you make new enemies here rather than bringing your old one's along."

"I understand."

"According to this latest entry," he said, "you don't actually understand." I clicked refresh on my browser and sure enough, it said, "Myron Oygold does not understand." I hung up, took off my clothes—except my North Face hat—and took two Xanax (2 MG). Then I got under my covers and settled into my bear trap life. Although, I had a dream about that little blue hummingbird.

New York City [edit]

The first time Myron Oygold applied to <u>New York City</u>, he was rejected.

When I woke up in my dark apartment, I saw my little sliver of sunlight pouring in the window, and I could tell it was morning. I had to pee, but I did not want to move. My phone rang. It was an area code I did not know, which filled me with anxiety. For the first time in months, I answered the call rather than leave it to voice mail. Naked, besides my hat, almost paralyzed with anxiety, my bladder about to break like a water balloon rolling down a summer driveway, I summoned the energy to click the speaker button. A little voice, distant yet chipper as a human resources specialist on your first day of work, said, "Was this all a game? A New Media experiment? An innovative way of testing the concepts of trust and accountability online?"

"Hello" I said.

"Is this Myron Oygold? I'm sorry. I got very excited after reading your Wikipedia page and your application. I haven't seen *anything* like it. This is Charlie Eisenbeg from the prestigious Florida Polytechnic University in Lakeland, Florida. I run the Awesome Media Lab over here, and I must say I am very impressed."

"Hello?"

"I don't know if you remember, but we met at the TPI Media Conference last October. I saw you present a paper on how the parents of newborn children will ultimately destroy Facebook. Cutting edge stuff. That evening, over dinner, you were the one who got drunk on Merlot. You were pacing and chain smoking, and you started to cry about your ex-girlfriend. Don't you remember?

"Please help me."

"You are a risk taker, and although I'm not completely convinced I actually like you as a person, your work is innovative, and you deserve a chance to teach here. So, what do you say, *Assistant Professor Oygold?*"

"Hello?"

Incompetence [edit]

Oygold once went to the pet store to buy a lolcat, but was disappointed to find out the truth, so he came home with a mouse named Jonathan who died during the ride home because Myron had put him in a plastic baggie like a fish. Myron then attempted to flush Jonathan down the toilet, but the water backed up, and Jonathan went spilling over the side as if it were a water park ride and washed up on the shore of the hallway. Horrified, Oygold slid a spatula underneath his wet, furry body, ran outside, and flung him into the neighbor's yard where his remains were toyed with by Hondo the cat who dragged the suffocated and drowned mouse around the yard by its tail for hours, as if Jonathan's body were an American soldier whose Blackhawk had crashed in Sudan. Jonathan was the only pet Oygold ever owned, and he only lived for two minutes.

They held graduation on the Old Quad. It was a warm spring day. The sky was the color of a blue Crayola crayon. My father took 17 photographs of me holding up my diploma. He told me he was proud of me and that he had recalculated my Life Success Probability. It was now a very respectable 50.5. My mother tweeted as I walked across the stage to receive my degree, *Myron looks so handsome in his doctoral robes! #oygold.*

Professor Smith-Smith waved to me from the crowd then dove back down into her iPad. She was sitting next to Samuel, who was wearing a black suit and a red tie that said RPI. He was grinning, but I couldn't read his expression. Was he happy for me? I took my diploma and shook the president's hand. Before I walked down the steps at the far end of the stage I looked past the neat rows of motor boards and golden tassels swaying like wind chimes, past the elm trees and old lamps at the edge of the Old Quad and past the ancient red brick of Sage Hall with its clinging, imported ivy. Standing next to one of the old lamps, I saw Ilana. It was probably some other girl with dark black hair and a beautiful Jewish nose, but I watched her linger for a moment. Was it her? It seemed like she was raising her hand but then quickly pulled it down, turned, and walked away.

Regrets [edit]

Oygold has a section on his resume called "Regrets" in which he lists, among other things, "The War of D.C.," "Grad School," and "Not Saying What I Needed to Say."

That evening, I checked my Wikipedia entry again. This was all that was written:

The Myth of Closure [edit]

An answer to a question that, long ago, Oygold asked someone:

"What are you? What are you to me? You are my gas station. My fireplace. My duct tape. You fill me up, keep me warm, hold me together. You are those little hand warmers they sell at the counter of country stores in Vermont in January. Resting my head on your belly under the blanket is the only place I ever felt safe. In you I seek shelter from my love for you. You are my bunker and my war."

The words lingered for a few weeks, but, like ancient symbols written on some distant shore, the digital tide eventually washed them out, and although the entry of Myron Oygold still exists, there are no words that I can see.

ABOUT THE AUTHOR

Jason Matthew Zalinger received his BA in English from the University of Connecticut, his MA in Media Ecology from New York University, and his PhD in Communication and Rhetoric from Rensselaer Polytechnic Institute. He has taught at a variety of institutions, including Rensselaer Polytechnic Institute, the University of South Florida, and Norwalk Community College. This is his first book, and he is very excited.

Printed in the United States
By Bookmasters